PATRONAGE
POLITICS
DIVIDES US

This research project was supported by:

PATRONAGE POLITICS DIVIDES US

A Study of Poverty, Patronage and Inequality in South Africa

Mcebisi Ndletyana,

Pholoana Oupa Makhalemele

Ralph Mathekga

MAPUNGUBWE
INSTITUTE FOR STRATEGIC REFLECTION (MISTRA)

MAPUNGUBWE
INSTITUTE FOR STRATEGIC REFLECTION(MISTRA)

Mapungubwe Institute for Strategic Reflection (MISTRA)
First floor, Cypress Place North
Woodmead Business Park
142 Western Service Road
Woodmead 2191
Johannesburg

First published November 2013

© MISTRA 2013

ISBN 978-1-920655-80-8

REAL AFRICAN PUBLISHERS

Published by Real African Publishers
on behalf of the Mapungubwe Institute for Strategic Reflection
(MISTRA)

First floor, The Mills
66 Carr Street
Newtown, Johannesburg 2001

Copy editor: Angela McClelland
Indexer: Jackie Kalley

Printed and bound in South Africa

MAPUNGUBWE INSTITUTE (MISTRA)
[A NON-PROFIT COMPANY][104-474-NPO]
REGISTRATION NUMBER 2010/002262/08
["THE INSTITUTE"]

CONTENTS

Foreword   6

Acknowledgements   8

Authors   10

List of Figures and Tables   11

Abbreviations   12

Chapter 1: Introduction   15

Chapter 2: Theoretical Framework   23

Chapter 3: Methodology   45

Chapter 4: Research Findings   61

Chapter 5: Analysis and Conclusions   113

Bibliography: 135

Index: 139

Foreword

D emocracy in South Africa's local communities has been nurtured over some 17 years. At the formal level, this has entailed the establishment of democratic local government structures and systems of accountability, processes of demarcation and re-demarcation, and the establishment of new administrations. As democratic local government matures, so have informal relationships between citizens and this sphere of government congealed – ranging from informal recruitment and employment practices, conduct of the councillors and municipal employees, and practices to garner political support and reward such, to local community protests.

The new local government structures are in large measure an antithesis of the illegitimate apartheid local authorities, which were fiercely resisted by the population. To this extent, they are also an extension of alternative expressions of people's power that started to manifest during the last decade of the apartheid system.

Nineteen years into democratic South Africa, however, it is apparent that this sphere of government is facing strain in many areas of the country. Numerous surveys, over different periods, indicate that local government is the least trusted of all spheres of government. Local protests over poor delivery of social services have become a recurrent feature in many communities. Structures and systems of accountability, such as ward committees and processes to develop integrated development plans (IDP), seem largely not to have delivered the initial promise.

It is against this backdrop that the Mapungubwe Institute (MISTRA) initiated research on *Poverty, Inequality and Patronage* as part of its first suite of eight Priority Research Projects. Through this research, MISTRA sought to gain insight into how patronage politics contributes to some of the problems being experienced; and further, how poverty and inequality articulate with such patronage.

In interrogating this correlation, the study does not seek to imply unique causality between poverty and inequality on the one hand and patronage politics on the other. Rather, it studies the concrete articulation among these dynamics as experienced by local communities. In pursuit of this objective, five diverse case studies were conducted in localities spread across four provinces. Researchers interviewed a number of individuals and interest groups, attended public meetings, and generally got a sense of life in these communities. The research was undertaken over a period of two years, about eight months of which were taken up by the fieldwork.

The process entailed numerous other activities including a series of colloquia with experts and recognised scholars in the field, and a peer review process.

The report goes beyond answering the primary questions of the study. It is a profile of socio-economic life in South Africa's various communities as experienced not only by locals, but also by foreign-born residents. The findings also show the relationship between councillors, business interests and local party organisations. While these issues are studied from the perspective of experiences in poor local communities, this does not necessarily imply the absence of patronage politics in areas where the well-off reside. The latter requires a separate study.

And so, what survivalist strategies do the poor adopt to manoeuvre the patronage minefield? How do they conduct themselves in relation to the often selective enforcement of municipal by-laws, which itself creates fertile ground for patronage and corruption? Where local residents come into conflict with foreign-born nationals or even with migrants from other parts of the country – is this reflective of a shared grievance among the majority? How do political parties discourage or entrench patronage politics and, in turn, what effect is this having on the parties themselves?

Communities' lived experiences, summarised in this report, do offer some answers to these questions. They contain many insights that suggest policy measures that can be undertaken by political parties and government structures to remedy the situation. The study distils these measures in the form of recommendations for consideration by policy makers. These range from internal party democracy in processes to select candidates for municipal elections, to the vexed question about the insidious impact of the current system of party political funding.

MISTRA is the first to acknowledge that this report does not drill deep enough into the core and related questions. We offer this study as part of a contribution to the necessary discussion that we should have about how to eliminate the negative effects of patronage politics, and thus strengthen South Africa's democracy.

We wish to extend our gratitude to the research team, including the field workers who, for extended periods, located themselves in these communities and trawled through masses of documentation arising from their interactions. We thank, too, the participants in workshops and colloquia, the peer reviewers and the donors for making this work possible.

Joel Netshitenzhe — Executive Director

ACKNOWLEDGEMENTS

A number of individuals and institutions, albeit to different degrees, contributed towards the successful completion of this research study. The researchers, Ralph Mathekga, Oupa Makhalemele, Khaya George, and Robert Gallagher deserve our greatest gratitude for the fieldwork and the numerous reports they wrote over a period close to a year. Their work benefitted and was ably guided by the core research team made up of Tony Trew, Karuna Mohan, Leslie Dikeni, and Mcebisi Ndletyana. Trew deserves special thanks for the overall leadership of the team and Dikeni for the eccentric, yet effective co-ordination of the team's activities.

We are grateful to the many community members, officials, and councillors for agreeing to do individual interviews and participate in focus group interviews. To avert possible harassment, some of the participants' names have been kept anonymous. They have been given pseudonyms instead.

A number of scholars, researchers, and interested individuals participated in a number of colloquia we convened to make sense of emerging research findings and to determine if researchers were on track. Here we are especially thankful to Professors Karl von Holdt, Anton Harber and Francis Wilson, and Mkhalelwa Mazibuko.

What follows below is not an exclusive product of the authors. Credit also goes to the editorial team, led by Joel Netshitenzhe, including Rachel Browne and Sedireng Lerakong, for their incisive comments and refinement of the initial drafts. The review of the final manuscript by Professor Xolela Mangcu only improved the final report. For that, we are thankful. The administrative and logistical support provided by MISTRA's Loyiso Ntshikila and Thabang Moerane proved invaluable throughout the entire research process. We would also like to extend our thanks to Yacoob Abba Omar, Director Operations, Gail Smith, Head of Communications and Outreach, and Linda Zwane, Communications Intern.

Most importantly, we would like to express our sincere appreciation to members of the reference team, who were quite instrumental in shaping this research project at inception. They include:

Johnny Steinberg; Khaya Ngema; Goolam Aboobaker, Seeraj Mohamed; Jacques Van Zuydam; Jenny Cargill; Prince Mashele; Brian King; Gino

Govender; David Monyae; Malose Langa, Benjy Mautjane; Paul von Hof, and Ephrem Tadesse.

As is customary in intellectual endeavours of this magnitude, without financial support, this report would not have been possible. The Olof Palme International Center and the Friedrich-Ebert-Stiftung deserve our special gratitude in this regard.

Though not directly involved with this research, MISTRA would nonetheless like to acknowledge its donors and funders for their support towards the Institute. They include:

Project Funders

- Friedrich-Ebert-Stiftung South Africa
- National Lottery Distribution Board
- Olof Palme International Center

MISTRA Funders

- Adcorp
- Ahanang Hardware and Construction
- Anglo Platinum
- Aveng
- Baswa
- Batho Batho Trust
- Brimstone
- Chancellor House Holdings
- Cyril Ramaphosa
- Darene Foundation
- De Beers Consolidated Mines Limited
- First Rand Foundation
- Ford Foundation
- Lincoln Mali
- Liphosa Matodzi
- Matemeku
- Mathews Phosa
- MTN Group
- Mvelaphanda Management Services
- Nedbank
- Ogilvy
- Roger Jardine
- Safika Holdings
- Sexwale Family Foundation
- Shanduka Group
- Simeka Group
- South African Breweries
- Standard Bank
- Transnet Foundation
- Yellowwoods

AUTHORS

Mcebisi Ndletyana
Head of Political Economy Faculty, Mapungubwe Institute for Strategic Reflection (MISTRA), South Africa.

Pholoana Oupa Makhalemele
Independent Research Consultant

Ralph Mathekga
Independent Research Consultant

LIST OF FIGURES AND TABLES

Figure 1	Map of South Africa Reflecting the Provinces	51
Figure 2	Employment Sector	62
Figure 3	Labour Force by Age	64
Figure 4	Labour Market	65
Figure 5	Monthly Household Income	67
Figure 6	Place of Birth	71
Figure 7	Households Energy for Cooking and Access to Piped Water	98
Figure 8	Enumeration Area Type	101
Table 1	Sites Selected for Observation	51

ABBREVIATIONS

AG	Auditor General
ALHDC	Affordable Land and Housing Data Centre
ANC	African National Congress
ANCYL	African National Congress Youth League
BGM	Branch General meetings
CCMA	Commission for Conciliation Mediation and Arbitration
CDW	Community Development Workers
CPF	Community Policing Forum
DA	Democratic Alliance
EXCO	Executive Council
FDI	Foreign Direct Investment
ID	Identity document
IDP	Integrated development planning
IFP	Inkatha Freedom Party
JDA	Johannesburg Development Agency
KANU	Kenya African National Union
LDF	Local Development Forum
LGESETA	Local Government Sector for Education and Training
MEC	Member of Executive Council
MOU	Memorandum of understanding
NFP	National Freedom Party
NGC	National General Council
NGO	Non-governmental organisation
NPM	New public management
PAN	Partido Accion Nacional (National Action Party)
PDR	Partido de la Revolución Democrática (Party of the Democratic Revolution)
PEC	Provincial Executive Committee
PHP	People's Housing Process
PR	Public relations
PRI	Partido Revolucionorio Institucional (Institutional Revolutionary Party)
RDP	Reconstruction Development Programme
REC	Regional Executive Committee
SANCA	South African Narcotics Association
SANCO	South African National Civic Organisation
SASSA	South African Social Security Agency
TEBA	The Employment Bureau of Africa
US	United States (of America)

CHAPTER 1

INTRODUCTION

A myriad of challenges continue to face the post-apartheid state. Some are of recent origin, birthed by conditions that arose in the wake of the democratic breakthrough. Yet other challenges straddle stubbornly across pre- and post-April 27 1994, defying the notion that the inaugural non-racial ballot heralded a watershed moment dividing the old from the new society, as if societal evolution can be packaged neatly into historical compartments.

Patronage politics has proven itself not only to be one such persistent challenge, but also a toxic kind. It is widespread, manifesting itself in the various sectors of our society, both public and private, as well as in various forms of organisation. Private companies are reportedly recipients of tenders awarded un-procedurally by politicians in exchange for a kickback. Some of the supposedly reputable business people become prominent donors to political parties, with implied conditionalities about benefits in return. Both the ruling party and the official opposition party, which is also a ruling party in some spheres of government, albeit ferociously disagreeing on numerous other issues, are congenially unanimous on non-disclosure of the identity of private donors to their respective parties.

Within the public sector, local government seems to be most afflicted by patronage politics. The Auditor General's audit report for the year 2010–2011, for instance, reveals a gloomy picture. Contracts worth R3.274 million were awarded to councillors and family members. Not only did councillors use their positions for self-enrichment, but a substantial number of people were employed into positions for which they were not qualified.[1]

The consequent damage is reflected in the audit performance of the municipalities. Only 5% of the municipal entities received a clean audit.

---

1. Auditor General Consolidated Report, 2010–2011.

While 17% of the auditees improved on their performance from the last financial year, 13% regressed. None of the municipalities in five provinces – Eastern Cape, Free State, Gauteng, Northern Cape, and North West – received any clean audit report, and, 10% of all municipalities have received a disclaimer or an adverse opinion for six years in succession.

Not only was the lack of appropriate skills a cause of poor audit performance, it is also the cause of additional wasteful expenditure. To make up for the lack of appropriate skills, municipalities have had to rely on consultants. Sixty-eight per cent of the municipal entities, which also includes development agencies, used consultants. This placed expenditure on consultants beyond R295 million. And the use of consultants had less to do with vacant posts, but more with a lack of expertise. Consultants were called in to assist even though municipalities had individuals employed to perform the very tasks for which they hired consultants.

Indeed, government's own municipal audits identified patronage politics as being at the core of municipal problems. The African National Congress (ANC), which controls more than two-thirds of the municipalities, has repeatedly lamented similar problems. For instance, the document titled 'Leadership renewal, discipline and organisational culture', discussed at the party's 2010 National General Council (NGC), notes that as early as 1997, at the Mafikeng Conference, the organisational report warned against leadership in the ANC being 'seen as a stepping-stone to positions of power and material reward in government and business'. The 2000 NGC remarked on 'disturbing trends of careerism, corruption and opportunism' creeping into the organisation. The 2002 Stellenbosch Conference 'raised concerns about members and branches being used as voting cattle and the tendency to have recruitment and active structures mainly for the purpose of elective conferences' (ANC, 'Leadership Renewal', 2002).

Patronage politics is not only a serious problem, it is also persistent. Consequently, community protests have not only been a frequent sight in our communities, but have also been violent. For instance, the second quarter of 2012 alone registered more service delivery protests, at 60, than 2011 (19) in the same period.[2] That was the highest number of protests registered within a quarter since 2004.

In response, government has introduced new legislation aimed specifically at addressing patronage politics. One such piece of legislation was the Municipal Systems Amendment Act, introduced in July 2011. The Act

---

2. Department of Co-operative Governance and Traditional Affairs, 'Service Delivery Protests: Trends from 2004 to June 2012'. A paper delivered at the ANC's Governance and Legislature Workshop, DBSA, Midrand, 17–18 August 2012.

prohibits employment of individuals in instances where no posts are available. And, where a post is available, especially for a municipal manager and a senior manager, it should be advertised nationally to ensure that it reaches the widest pool of people possible, thus increasing the likelihood of attracting the best candidate for the post. Moreover, the new Act bars local party office bearers from holding municipal positions simultaneously. It is not clear yet if this law has achieved its intended results.

Studying patronage politics is thus paramount. The phenomenon has implications for the performance of local government and the vibrancy of South African democracy. Violent protests, which are caused partly by malfunctioning municipalities and corrupt councillors, are of great concern. In some instances, they disrupt municipal functioning and destroy crucial public assets, rather than add impetus to service delivery. This, and other related concerns, makes this research study into patronage politics fundamentally important.

Accordingly, the study examined patronage politics within the context of local government. Local government provides an apt setting. It is both a direct implementer of government programmes as well as the nearest point of government contact with the citizenry. This sphere of governance allows for both a reasonable measurement of government impact on the lives of people, and to discern the nature and impact of government-citizenry interactions.

This study thus has sought not only to gain deeper insight into the causes, manifestation, and impact of patronage politics, but also to examine how official measures at curbing the phenomenon have fared. In other words, the aims are to understand the specific nature and various forms of patronage politics; the conditions under which it thrives (or disappears); and its specific impact on the structures of governance, political culture and the citizenry.

Specifically, the study examined how patronage politics articulates with conditions of poverty. While not assuming causality between poverty and patronage in either direction, the study examines whether the prevalence of patronage in specific communities has anything to do with the fact that poor people are less organised or unable to access state services independent of the corrupt intermediary of public officials. If indeed it was so, the study then set out to probe how poor people could best respond to these challenges.

Equally critical for the study was the institution of the party system. It ponders the ways in which a party could be constituted in a manner that forecloses the flourishing of patronage politics, and sought to identify the conditions under which a political party may be able to cure itself of the pathology of patronage politics. The overall aim of the study, therefore, was to explore the possibility of constituting public institutions in a manner that enables them to become legitimate arbiters between the various interests, rather than as instruments that are captured by contending interest groups for their own accumulation.

Most importantly, this study was necessitated by the realisation that post-apartheid patronage politics has not received sufficient scholarly attention. Other than the official reports by government and conference documents by the ruling party, there is a general paucity of scholarly material on this subject. This research study aims to help fill that gap, especially by contributing empirical research to the subject.

The study was informed by a number of assumptions. It assumed that the presence or saliency of patronage politics hinges on the socio-economic context and the responsiveness of public institutions to the citizenry. The extent to which individuals are prone to engage in patronage politics is determined by extant socio-economic status and aspirations of socio-economic advancement. Oftentimes such individuals do not have any other means or alternative sources of income, leaving patronage politics as the primary source of livelihood or material advancement.

That ordinary citizens are susceptible to personal persuasions to vote in return for material rewards is equally a commentary on how they perceive or relate to state institutions. They do not trust that public institutions will provide them what is, in some cases, their entitlement arising from their citizenship. Rather, they rely on personal ties with individual politicians or officials as a guarantee.

Popular distrust of state institutions is in turn a product of South Africa's specific history of racial discrimination and oppression. Specifically, it stems from years of systematic neglect by officialdom. Black people especially became sceptical of the responsiveness of public institutions to their plight.

In the face of an uncaring bureaucracy, or without any recourse, people have resorted to approaching individuals within the state institutions. The public officials, in turn, have taken advantage of people's vulnerability, demanding payment in return for the services. In this instance, patron-client relations develop a countermeasure to the indifference of the officialdom.

Not only does the official indifference generate public scepticism, it also leads to insecurity. This is particularly so in communities where there is no official presence, or where communities are not within reach of the public institutions. In other words, such communities are on the margins of society, with their residents vulnerable to abuse or needy of certain services that are otherwise provided by the State. 'Strong men' thus emerge to provide either security or services in exchange for payment. This was particularly common in South Africa's informal settlements, which were totally ignored by the State (White, 1993).

Patronage politics, though a product of existing circumstances, is therefore also an offshoot of a long existing public culture that is rooted in South African history and developed as a response to the unresponsiveness of the apartheid public institutions to the needs of black people. 'Strong men' became such public institutions. The taxi industry and the Mashonisa (loan sharks) are but a few examples of institutions that evolved around 'strong men' to provide what black people could not secure from the apartheid state and financial institutions. The functioning of such 'institutions' is personalised, subject to the moods of the person.

A function of the party system, patronage politics, is also indicative of the weakness of the party. Reports by the ruling party indicate that dispensers of patronage are known, but nothing is done to rein them in. Such individuals may be considered too important to the popularity of the party in a particular community, and thus any punitive actions against them may alienate support for the party. This suggests that the party relies more on personal appeals than the strength of its ideology and record. The fear could be that the party as a brand is weak, and that it requires to be vouched for by local notables, who are essentially gatekeepers, without whom the party cannot get support.

Evidently, patronage is inadequate as a foundation upon which to build a democratic state. The ruling party or public sector only has a limited number of vacancies for party worker placement. Party loyalists exceed the number of public sector jobs available. This may nudge the ruling party into striking a deal with the private sector to provide jobs for its cadres in exchange for some benefits. The State becomes a 'rentier state'.

In instances where party loyalists cannot get jobs anywhere else, institutional instability is the likely result. South Africa's ruling party, the ANC, as noted earlier, has in fact ascribed municipal instability, characterised by a constant change of office bearers and firing of public officials, to 'careerism' – a phenomenon that is also known as the '*dedel abanye* principle' (make way for others). Party loyalists that are either unemployed or not elected to public office use their influence within the party to get others removed so that they can replace them (ANC, 3rd NGC, SG's Organisational Report, 2010).

Support gained through patronage is also tenuous. Once patronage dries up, so will the support for the individual leaders or the party. Change of economic fortunes, therefore, is likely to disrupt the party's ability to provide patronage. Parties in such situations have resorted to dictatorship to retain power. Patronage, as an instrument of eliciting support, is best treated as a short-term measure that may disappear at any time, leaving the party without any support. It is useful as an immediate, legitimising tool, but can also be counter-productive in the long-run.

Experiences from elsewhere, however, suggest that electoral competition can nudge a reluctant party towards ridding itself of patronage seekers, for patronage politics yields bad governance, which in turn threatens the very popularity of the party. Faced with possible ascendancy of rival parties, a political party is likely to reform in order to retain (or gain) political office.

The study was pursued through qualitative methodology. Specifically, researchers conducted interviews with individuals and groups of individuals, and also engaged focus groups. Moreover, a case study approach was used, selecting five research sites, spread out in four of South Africa's provinces, namely the Western Cape, Eastern Cape, Gauteng, and Free State. Fieldwork was conducted over a period of approximately 18 months beginning around October 2010 and ending in July 2012. Focus group interviews followed in the last half of 2012.

The research report has five chapters. What follows is a theoretical framework. Here the report provides an exhaustive definition of patronage politics, showing especially its relationship to poverty. The chapter goes beyond theory to account for the historical origin of patronage politics, sketching out how this phenomenon has played itself out in various historical contexts and countries. Thereafter, there is a chapter on methodology. The chapter not only explains the methodology adopted for the study, but also accounts for why it was chosen. Included in the methodology chapter are challenges that researchers encountered in the course of fieldwork and focus group interviews, and the lessons that such experiences provided for researchers in general. A chapter containing research findings follows. The findings, presented thematically, drawing from the various case studies, are structured into six sections. The final chapter provides an analysis of the research findings and concludes the report. Included in the chapter are policy recommendations that attempt to contribute towards curbing the corrosive impact of patronage on local politics. Where problems do not lend themselves to policy correction, they are nonetheless highlighted to underscore the urgency to address them.

CHAPTER 2

THEORETICAL FRAMEWORK

Patronage is a topical subject in South Africa, synonymous in the media with exposés of corrupt government officials, and often cited along with the so-called 'cadre deployment' as one of the biggest problems characterising the ruling party's government. Its critics accuse the ANC of relying too heavily on political patronage, to the extent that it compromises its own governance record and its ability to make good on its electoral injunction to build a better life for all.

In townships around South Africa (notably historically black townships characterised by high levels of abject poverty and backlogs in infrastructure development), public unrest has flared up, ostensibly to force the authorities (be they the local municipality, provincial, or national government) to intervene in what communities consider to be poor levels of service delivery by their respective local governments. The local leadership of these protest actions explain that the violence that characterises them is a deliberate strategy to force the authorities to listen to their grievances. These grievances often revolve around allegations of official corruption and favouritism, and are often aimed at removing officials whose bona fides the locals do not accept, as they feel the latter are imposed upon them 'from the top' or have failed to fulfil the promises for which they were elected.

At another level these protests expose some hard truths about local government. One is that they expose the lack of faith in the various institutions at the local level designed to give voice to residents in their own governance; research has also shown that sometimes the protests are instigated by protagonists in the intrigues of intraparty rivalries (see von Holdt, 2011). It is also believed that the authority exercised by political parties in the deployment of individuals to act as representatives at the local government level sometimes takes away the residents' prerogative to elect their own people, with the result that local representatives are accountable more to those who deployed them than to the residents in whose name they govern.

The broad consensus holds that political patronage happens when state resources are used to reward individuals in return for their electoral support. Perceptions and understandings of patronage are often value-laden, as patronage is considered immoral, and is often associated with practices whereby appointments to public office or government resources and contracts are disbursed to undeserving, incompetent individuals. Yet patronage is much more ubiquitous and has manifested in many different ways.

Fukuyama (2011) points out that in each case where politicians draw support from patron-client ties to get elected to parliament:

> ...the underlying social relationship between the politician and his or her supporters is the same as in a kinship group: it is based on a reciprocal exchange of favours between leader and followers, where leadership is won rather than inherited, based on the leader's ability to advance the interests of the group (Fukuyama, 2011, p. 79).

Patronage politics expresses itself within a patron-client relationship and cuts across historical periods. Before the onset of democratic systems of government, patronage politics was in essence the foundation of state legitimacy and control. In recent times it became more sophisticated with the onset of the party system, by virtue of the fact that political parties seek control of the State and, through the latter, gain control over resources. To underscore the stubbornness of patronage politics well within the modern political milieu, Fukuyama reminds us that in American cities 'political machines are built up on the basis of who scratches whose back and not some "modern" motivation like ideology or public policy' (Fukuyama, ibid.).

In Medieval Europe, feudalism christened patronage politics as a reciprocal relationship: an exchange of services and goods between the 'haves' and the 'have-nots'. It enabled one to get from the other what s/he did not have – a practice that anthropologists called 'generalised exchange'. The landlord provided a vassal with a piece of land on which to eke out subsistence in exchange for labour, a share of his produce, or military skills (Hosking, 2000). Other clients entered into the relationship to secure protection within what was otherwise a volatile environment, where the rule of law was not institutionalised or public administration was not bureaucratised.

What became a common feature of patronage politics within the modern state, which we discuss later, was inaugurated under feudal rule. Imperial rulers, in lieu of salaries, paid local officials in kind. This even entailed turning a blind eye to the latter's solicitation of favours from the subject population. In the absence of a clearly defined system of the rule of law, where arbitrary decrees were not uncommon under erratic local administrators, locals also found offers of patronage to the officialdom a useful protection against victimisation. Hosking (2000) put it thus: 'In these circumstances, law was not a complex of mutually binding rights and obligations, but took the form of command from above, reinforced by peer pressure (p. 308).'

In lieu of salaries from the royal court, imperial officials considered patronage just payment for their administrative duties. Ultimately, it was abuse of public office to extract favours. The only difference, though, from how patronage politics subsequently came to be practiced, was that it did not necessarily discard merit (Hosking, 2000). Equally critical to reiterate is that it mushroomed under conditions of disorder, where law was not institutionalised and administration not based upon bureaucratic principles.

DEMYSTIFYING PATRONAGE: UNDERSTANDING ITS DIFFERENT MANIFESTATIONS

Bearfield (2009), on the other hand, cites various previous studies on experiences of patronage in the United States, noting at the outset the paucity of research in the area, outlining different applications of patronage, and debunking some of the assumptions held by most of those who talk about patronage. Bearfield cites a 1950s study done by Frank Sorauf, of a rural county in Pennsylvania, US that shows that patronage, while used as a political tool by some in political power, took different forms and served other ends, too. He notes that in the study Sorauf 'revealed that the patronage system was used as an ad hoc merit system, whereby skilled and experienced men were recruited by superintendents and caretakers and then given even a semblance of tenure regardless of political changes' (Bearfield, 2009, p. 64).

In the main, though, Sorauf points out that the onset of the party system transformed patronage politics. 'Patronage has for long remained a tail tied to the kite of a party; once its importance to a party was conceded, its fortune rose with that of the party. To attack patronage was to challenge the party and appear to be burning the barn to kill the mice'(Sorauf, 1959, p.116).' Patronage came to be dispensed by the leadership of the political party, and beneficiaries included both party loyalists/cadres as well as the voters of the party. The catalyst was not so much the introduction of the party system, but more the imperative to win elections. Political parties contested elections and, in order to win, needed to build a majority on their side. The promise and the actual handing out of patronage became the tool to first, build an effective party machinery to mount an effective election campaign and turn out voters on election-day, and second, to convince voters to cast their ballots in favour of the party. Thus Sorauf (1960) defines patronage as an *incentive system* – 'a political currency with which to purchase political activity and political responses' (p. 28).

Though effectively instrumentalising political activism, the initial onset of political parties, however, had a progressive effect and was impelled by a normative objective. Andrew Jackson's political party, a dominant feature of American politics between 1829 and 1861, for instance, heralded the onset of mass-based politics in the US. It was a (progressively) radical movement. Before it burst onto America's political scene, public office was considered a preserve of the American elite: those who had distinguished themselves through education and wealth. The Jacksonian movement opened up service in the State to ordinary folk regardless of social background or standing. Jackson demystified public office, arguing that, as Scott (2000) puts it: '...administrative responsibilities were capable of being made "so simple and plain" that any citizen of normal capacity could readily perform the public work' (p. 17).

Albeit enticing support with the offer of a job in the public sector, Scott contends (ibid) the Jacksonian movement was nonetheless redistributive in character. It rotated public sector jobs to as many party loyalists as possible. One could only hold down a job in the public service for a limited period of four years, and thereafter make way for other fellow party loyalists. The idea was to enable as many people as possible to get jobs, rather than limiting them to a few individuals within the party. Perhaps even more noteworthy was that by drawing massive numbers into the electoral process, the Jacksonian movement both nurtured and spread democratic culture. Material gain was not an end in itself, but an instrument to a normative, objective, civic mindedness (see also Schlesinger, 1945).

Scott (2000) suggests that material inducement was justified. The general American populace at the time suffered from an anti-party and anti-organisational political culture. Material inducement acted as a solvent. If not for their conviction in parties, then ordinary folk were enticed into party organisation by the promise of rewards. But once they were within the fold of the party and participated in the electoral process, party recruits learnt to become civic minded.

The Jacksonian movement saw the party itself as an institution of civic education, in the same vein as the public school and popular press. Party activism cultivated patriotism, shared values, and promoted awareness about public issues. Party membership and service in the public office provided ordinary folk with tangible experience in what were essentially abstract republican ideas. The prospect of material reward, therefore, served to break the initial resistance to party involvement, and while serving in the party and in the public service, citizens would eventually become civic minded.

But the principle of job rotation also yielded unintended results for the Jacksonian movement. Though successful in recruiting new members, it could not sustain the loyalty of old members. Since an administrative job was held on a rotational basis, it was unlikely that one would hold it twice, and one would have to wait for a considerably long period to get another job. Old members, who had completed their four-year employment period in public administration, were thus discouraged from remaining loyal to the party.

The high turnover of members, therefore, coupled with the increasing competitiveness of the electoral contests, was to transform the 'pure-and-simple-spoils party' that characterised the Jacksonian movement, into a political machine in the 1870s.

It is worthwhile reiterating that the change in political context – i.e. competitive elections – served as a catalyst, reconfiguring the nature of the political party, the manner in which patronage was dispensed, as well as the objective of party recruitment. It became critical for parties to have an experienced core of cadres that would campaign and turn out voters for the party. The emphasis thus shifted from rotating to retaining members because of their experience and knowledge of how the party functioned. Thus, a political party, as a political machine, was born with patronage as the main instrument of recruitment, engendering at times, adverse results on the nature of politics and quality of governance.

A political machine is a well organised, elaborate and hierarchical structure. The party is defined by a widespread organisational network, patterned along the geographic spread of the country and staffed by committed party activists at different levels. Local leaders assume the character of a 'boss' with a posse of cadres under their charge. Patronage is allocated on the basis of votes that a 'boss' brings to the party. Those who perform impressively are rewarded, while those who do not deliver the votes are simply replaced. The machine is geared towards vote-maximisation – the idea being that the clients bring in votes for the party in exchange for spoils. Supporters thus become lifelong members of the party with a stake in maintaining it in power so as to keep their jobs. They become devoted to the party because it is the source of their livelihood (Sorauf, 1960, & Wilson, 1961).

A political machine of this kind, therefore, is essentially an instrument of accumulation. Members are enticed to the party, as noted earlier, purely by the offer of material benefits. They are not bound to the party by any ideological ties or commitment to a particular programme. The party is preoccupied with capturing power, and party workers are attracted to it by the material benefits it awards them. Political activism is reduced to material indulgence or gain. The political machine therefore operates on a principle of reciprocity, e.g. votes in return for a job. In other words, as Scott (1969) explains, the party:

…relies on what it accomplishes in a concrete way for its supporters, not on what it stands for. A machine may in fact be likened to a business in which all members are stockholders and dividends are paid in accordance with what has been invested (p. 144).

Patronage is thus critical to the functioning of the party. Where ideological conviction is absent, patronage keeps the party intact. It can be harnessed to promote intra-party cohesion, enticing dissident local party leaders or factions back under the discipline and hierarchy of the party leadership. It has also been used to finance the party itself. Party appointees would pay a certain percentage of their salaries to the party (Sorauf, 1960).

If the intensity of electoral competition injected the initial impetus towards patronage politics, conditions of poverty and marginality made it prosper:

Machines characteristically thrive on suffrage of the poor, and, naturally, prosper best when the poor are many and the middle-class few …

Poverty shortens a man's time horizon and maximises the effectiveness of short-run material inducements ... Attachments to policy goals or to an ideology imply something of a future orientation as well as wide loyalties, while poverty discounts future gains and focuses unavoidably on the here and now (Scott, 1969, p. 150).

Thus, according to Scott, patronage politics is most likely to thrive under conditions of poverty and poor access to skills and opportunities.

Moynihan and Wilson (1964, cited in Bearfield, 2009) characterise this practice in the United States as 'recognition' of members of a minority or racial group by a dominant party (or one of the dominant parties). A party appoints members of a minority group to political office as a way of demonstrating that it recognises the group, and in turn gets their votes. Szeftel (2000) notes a similar phenomenon. Employing the concept of clientelism, Szeftel notes how recruitment from networks of support is not only a way of organising societies, but serves also the role of rendering the currently marginalised more visible and audible:

...clientelism has proved to be an effective means both of giving a democratic voice to the demands of those previously marginalised, and of enabling propertied classes to legitimate their political dominance (Szeftel, 2000, p. 430).

The offer of a job in exchange for party activism is evidently difficult to resist, particularly when employment opportunities are very limited, a situation exacerbated when party supporters make claims to jobs by invoking autochthony to legitimise these claims over minorities or immigrant populations in times of high unemployment (Neocosmos, 2011). Jobs thus gained have a precarious tenure, though, as the new governing party terminates the services of the loyalists of the defeated rival party and brings its own party loyalists into state employment.

The spoils of victory also extend to the specific communities that supported the party. 'Pork-barrel projects' (or public works programmes), whose necessity is not always apparent, are initiated with the clear intention of providing employment to that community. This is what makes patronage politics, according to Sorauf, 'the politics of the underprivileged' (Sorauf, 1960, p. 31). Nonetheless, it is not farfetched to conclude, as Johnston (1979) does, that at some level patronage politics bridges 'social divisions by seeking money from the affluent and votes from the poor' (ibid., p. 385). It facilitates social mobility of marginal classes that would otherwise remain on the margins of society.[1]

It is critical to note, though, as Scott (1969) reminds us, that patronage politics is not peculiar to poor people. The middle and upper classes also vote for a party in return for certain rewards. Whereas patronage among the poor and immigrant communities might take the form of material rewards, such as pork-barrel projects or public works and employment, the middle to upper income groups might be enticed to vote in return for a promise of promulgating a particular legislation and policy, thus advancing their own 'class' interests. The legislation may entail tax concessions or subsidies. The benefit, although legal in a technical sense, could nonetheless have a perverse effect on governance. Appointments may be made mainly in pursuit of said benefits, and these classes have been known to tolerate a corrupt government. Albeit without immediately perceivable corrosive effects on governance, patronage politics in this incarnation tends to perpetuate inequality. That is particularly true of political parties or politicians that are wholly dependent on business donations for their election campaigns. Once in parliament or government, they become lobbies or proxies for private business, sponsoring or promulgating legislation that adversely affects the poor and working class communities.

PATRONAGE AS A SOCIAL GOOD?

Although limited to events in the US, Bearfield's article contains insights that resonate with experiences in South Africa and Kenya – the example of 'Reform Patronage' being instructive. Mwayi Kibaki led a successful coalition campaign in Kenya which ousted Daniel Arap Moi, who for decades had presided over a corrupt government on an anti-corruption ticket. Kibaki, as the new president of Kenya, promptly commenced a programme targeted at ending government corruption, for which he relied firmly on his patronage networks, appointing key individuals from the campaign and also from civil society. Although Kibaki failed to withstand the exigencies of incumbency, and the programme was derailed with its lofty goals, it should be acknowledged that, at least initially, he used patronage for a positive agenda.

Charles van Onselen, in *New Babylon, New Nineveh* (1982), gives some detail of the President of the Transvaal Republic, Paul Kruger's active role in

---

1. For further insight, *see also* Freedman, 1988 & Gump, 1971.

using patronage to protect the interests of *boer* famers, some Afrikaner entrepreneurs, as well as personal friends, by thwarting plans of industrialists and financiers (including overseas based ones) who were seeking to capitalise on the gold rush in the Witwatersrand in the late 1890s and early 1900s, and thus manipulated the situation to subvert chances of the *buitelanders'* dominance. In return, Kruger sought continued loyal support from the boers engaged in agriculture who were concerned about their interests being under threat of the new, more worldly players in the Witwatersrand.[2]

The thrust of Bearfield's article is an appeal for an understanding of patronage qua patronage, and to desist from seeing the phenomenon as pathology, an evil to be rooted out, but rather as a tool for organising society. It ought to be acknowledged and understood for what it is. Considered a tool, it can, and has been, used in subversive ways. But it can also, as it has been, be used for positive ends. Kopecky notes: 'Patronage conceived as a form of control can…denote a type of state exploitation in the literal sense of the word, more in the spirit of use and management than of misuse and mistreatment' (Kopecky, 2011, p. 728).

Scott (1969) asserts that patronage, especially in developing countries, has a legitimising effect. Newly independent, post-colonial states especially, suffered from a lack of popular democratic culture. Democratic ideas were not entrenched in public culture, nor were they widely shared by the populace. The promise of patronage induced an otherwise uninterested citizenry into the electoral process, and established legitimacy for the new democratic state.

INEQUALITY AND PATRONAGE: ECHOES FROM THE PAST

South Africa is probably the most unequal society in the world today. Leibbrant and Finn, in their rigourous comparative study to measure inequalities between South Africa and Brazil, conclude that while Brazil has over the past decade succeeded to decrease inequality, inequality in South Africa has over the same period increased (Leibbrant & Finn, 2012). These inequalities are bound to be perpetuated over time, and they mirror the demographic composition of the apartheid era the current government is entrusted with dismantling.

Reporting on a World Bank study of South Africa's economy, journalist Mmenyane Seoposengwe surmises thus:

---

2. See also Hyslop, J. (2005) *Political Corruption: Before and After Apartheid, A Journal of Southern African Studies*, Vol. 31, Number 4, December 2005.

South Africa's weak performance on providing employment opportunities is hampered not only by slow job creation but also by a highly unequal access to the limited number of opportunities. Global comparisons show South Africa to be an outlier in terms of both the level and inequality of employment opportunities. **The employment situation is especially challenging for the younger labour force, residents of townships/informal settlements and rural areas, and the non-white (sic) segments of the population** (Emphasis added) (Seoposengwe, M. (2012): press release – www.worldbank.org).

She goes on to say:

A key message of this report is that not only is it important from [a] policy perspective to know **how many** *people are being excluded from basic service provision but also* **who** *is being excluded and whether that systematically reflects a particular set of circumstances (such as ethnicity, gender, location of birth and family background) that are beyond an individual's control* (emphasis in original) (Seoposengwe, M. (2012): press release – www.worldbank.org).

That inequality persists so many years after the liberation in South Africa puts the incumbent government under tremendous pressure to fulfil its mission of ending these inequalities. Liberation movements in Africa, having earned the trust, and embodying the hopes of nascent post-colonial African nations, took over the reins of post-colonial governments with a resounding mandate from the populace to commence the task of undoing the impoverishment and inequalities left in the wake of the departing administration. The motivation to address inequality is therefore strong. Far more important than to please the masses, these liberators should, by mere force of logic, see it as being in their interest to redress inequality. The State, over and above interventions it can pursue to this end, can at least provide conditions that allow for economic growth and human development.

Besley and Maitreesh (2006) argue that weak public goods provision disproportionately hurts the poor. For example, the free market (as it has been clearly demonstrated in South Africa) allows wealthy individuals to access resources such as water, sanitation, healthcare, transportation, and schools; yet, it is inadequate for supplying these goods to the needy. Furthermore, because of the resultant lack of skills, infrastructure, and general human development, such societies are bound to lose out on foreign direct investment (even despite relatively lower wages) to comparatively more attractive regions of the globe (such as East Asia and the Pacific for example) where there are better levels of human capital.

In his study on patronage in sub-Saharan Africa, Kroeger (2012) cites a selection of studies that show that greater investment in human capital, coupled with adequate provision of public goods, have a significant impact on growth and development. Citing the growth theory in Solow (1957), Kroeger concurs with the notion that the technological innovation resulting from research and development, a spillover from FDI in manufacturing, have had a positive impact on the productivity of indigenous Chinese firms.

> *If Sub-Saharan Africa is ever able to reap similar benefits, increases in public goods are a necessity to increase the human capital and infrastructure necessary to attract higher levels of FDI* (Kroeger, 2012, p. 14–15).

Besley and Maitreesh (2006) point out that the political elite on the continent, instead of promoting growth and human development by providing important public goods such as education, public health, and so on, tend to place greater focus on diverting public revenue to a select group of constituents.

So what is holding the African post-colonial and post-apartheid state back? Several scholars have suggested that the apple has not fallen far from the tree. Crawford Young employs a zoological analogy: 'In metamorphosis the caterpillar becomes a butterfly without losing its inner essences' (Crawford Young, 2004, p. 2). Thus, the post-colonial state retains the colonial state's DNA. Morris Szeftel (2000) in an instructive reflection on clientelism and corruption and their unique manifestations in Africa, points out that while it is important to control corruption as an element of legitimating liberal democracy, it is much more critical to understand the way in which clientelist forms of political mobilisation have 'promoted corruption and intensified [the] crisis' (Szeftel, 2000, p. 427). This crisis comes about in the wake of anti-corruption efforts whose design has had the effect of stifling the prerogative of controlling and appropriating state resources by incumbent governments as trade-offs with donor countries, to allow the flow of such aid (ibid, p. 427).

Szeftel argues that although widespread in Africa, high-level corruption is not markedly worse than in many other parts of the 'Third Wave' entrants into democracy (for example in Eastern Europe). In fact, he argues, the sums involved in this high-level corruption in Africa, are puny in comparison to the latter region.

> Yet corruption in Africa is universally perceived ... as being 'catastrophic' in its impact on development, a major cause (in the eyes of some, even the main cause) of economic crisis, authoritarianism, political instability and state collapse (Szeftel, 2000).

According to Szeftel, corruption is more a symptom than a cause of crisis in Africa. Where we see corruption, we should be on the lookout for much deeper problems. In dealing with corruption, Szeftel contends, it is important to challenge the link between corruption, on the one hand, and patterns of private accumulation and clientelist political mobilisation, on the other. Measures brought about by donor agents in order to curb corruption only tend to deepen the crisis if they do not make adequate appraisal of these nuances.

> Moreover, because they interfere with patterns of private accumulation and political patronage, and threaten the privileges which state office bestows on political elites and their supporters and associates, [anti-corruption measures] create problems in the relationship between donor and debtor governments and are bitterly resented and resisted by ruling elites (Szeftel, 2000, p. 428).

Like Fanon (1961) and Neocosmos (2011), Szeftel points out the role assumed by the new middle class in post-colonial Africa in transferring public resources to itself and the bourgeois strata as it emerges.

Dismissing widely-held assumptions about the causes of corruption in sub-Saharan Africa (including notions like 'the politics of the belly', 'big man', and so on), Szeftel reveals a clear link between corruption and its manifestations in post-colonial Africa to the departing colonial system the former is seeking to replace.

Elsewhere, Szeftel (1987) expands on the nature of the colonial state and its impact on the shape of the post-colonial African state. The former colonies, out of which the new African state is emerging, were nothing much beyond being repositories and conveyors of primary goods for export to the international markets, thus entrenching these countries in a wider, international division of labour where their dependency on fluctuating market forces conspired with other factors to under develop the region. The situation led to uneven development.

> *Uneven development took many forms, among them: the combination of declining peasant subsistence economies with multinational export production; extreme inequalities of income; the differential incorporation of different regions and ethnic groups into the colonial economy and state; and the exclusion of vast numbers of Africans from property ownership, capital, skills and market opportunities though institutionalised racism* (Szeftel, 1987).

With this legacy and the market forces thus stacked up against the African post-colonial state, and particularly considering that these market forces were dominated by foreign powers and characterised by racism, political power was the only viable avenue for private accumulation as well as for development (Szeftel, 2000, p. 431).

> *The conjuncture of colonial exclusion, nationalist promises and political independence produced almost limitless expectations of government to intervene in the economy, to redistribute entitlements and to provide jobs, loans, contracts and favours through political patronage* (Szeftel, 1987, p. 118).

These states had inherited the colonial administrations, whose *raison d'être* was, as described above, to ensure order in furthering the facilitation of the export of commodities. The colonial state was not, in other words, concerned with establishing institutions necessary to develop the local polity in any way other than the furtherance of the metropole's accumulation plans. Mamdani in his seminal work, *Citizen and Subject* (1996), shows how state institutions in the colonial system served this role. Reserving civil rights to the urban, white expatriates from the homeland, the colonial administration set up traditional authorities to lord over mostly rural-based indigenous populations, excluding them from civil freedoms.

The post-colonial African state therefore inherited a colonial state configured not for the development of the local society, while inheriting its authoritarian style. Importantly, it set up the enabling social structures for patronage networks when it retained the rural-urban dichotomy which was itself set along ethnic lines.

It is important to acknowledge the existence of the State in pre-colonial Africa, and to see how Europeans subverted political institutions to their own ends. Basil Davidson (1991), Francis Fukuyama (2011), and Mahmood Mamdani (1996) show how political order was arranged across different African polities over many centuries prior to Europeans' ventures into the continent. These polities were based on familial, ethnic or religion-based ties and identities. In order to facilitate accumulation on behalf of the metropoles, colonial authorities usurped traditional leaders in such societies (sometimes going as far as installing their preferred 'tribal leaders'), and redeployed them to rule by proxy on behalf of the colonial administration (Mamdani, ibid.). In South Africa, these traditional leaders would later be co-opted as leaders of the *bantustans* as the apartheid government consolidated its policy of keeping South Africa 'white'.

In South Africa, the Bantustan system created a huge bureaucracy (more than 600 000-strong across South Africa) distinguished for deficiencies in technical and managerial capacity, corruption, and laxity in adherence to formal procedures (Gibbs, 2011). A culture of patronage was entrenched as people drew on personal networks, notably usurped by those in the bureaucracy and traditional leadership (ibid.).

Hyslop shows how, during the transitional period in the early 1990s, the ANC found itself faced with the realities of insufficient numbers of properly trained cadres to fill the administrative posts and reluctantly conceded to the logic of gaining the support of the black middle-class administrators of the homelands (Hyslop, 2005). Furthermore, Picard (2005) points out how the former homeland administrators assumed a strong bargaining position, entering alliances with the white, apartheid civil service in seeking job security in the new administration.

Thus these apartheid-era administrators, with their entrenched networks of patronage, effectively incubated a culture wherein post-apartheid administrators have simply 'stepped in to play a role in political and economic brokering for poor, local communities' (Chipkin and Meny-Gibert, 2012, p. 108).

Chipkin and Meny-Gibbert (ibid.) suggest that, while the national departments in Pretoria during apartheid could be characterised as bureaucratic, law-driven, hierarchical, multi-layered, departmentally fragmented, inward-orientated, and a racial oligarchy, their counterparts in the former homelands functioned more through informal procedure and networks, than a rule-driven hierarchy.

Energised by the desire to create a modern bureaucracy, the new government sought to change the orientation of the State into an innovative and adaptive public service that could respond to 'increasingly globalised and complex societies' (ibid., p. 109). A number of public sector reform initiatives thus followed under the rubric New Public Management (NPM). Chipkin and Meny-Gibbert point out, however, that the NPM 'took too little cognisance of recent history, especially the nature of former homeland administrations' (ibid.), echoing Szeftel's warning that without a robust appraisal of the entrenched culture, orientation, and tendencies (stubbornly outliving the past administration), the State's attempt of moving forward is hampered.

Pointing out these deficiencies in the democratising effort should not be confused with cynicism. There is a clear need for supporting democratic ethos. Post-colonial African states proved especially vulnerable to ethnic manipulation by wily politicians. Leaders often manipulated the vacuum left by the colonial administrators to subvert 'self-determination' of the people. They targeted a majority ethnic group, giving them preferred treatment over the rest, in return for their bloc votes. And voters did not necessarily hold them accountable. Politicians thus behaved as they wished, even abusing public office. Material benefits were sufficient for voters to repeatedly return what were, in most cases, inept and corrupt politicians back to political office.[3]

Patronage has been so ensconced in the sinews of the system that it seemed that parties would not function without it. At least that is what America's George Washington Plunkitt, a prominent New York-based politician in the late nineteenth century to early twentieth century, believed:

> First, this great and glorious country was built up by the political parties; second, parties can't hold together if their workers don't get the offices when they win; third, if the parties go to pieces, the government they built up must go to pieces, too; fourth, then there'll be h—l to pay (Sorauf, 1959, p. 116).

A considerable volume of scholarship, however, dismisses the assumed permanency of the party-patronage nexus. The saliency of patronage in

---

3. *See also* Mwenda and Tangri, 2005.

politics can easily wane, because, according to Sorauf (1959), it is 'not a universal concomitant of the political process; it is rooted deeply in a particular set of social conditions and traditions' (ibid., p. 118). A change in the socio-economic context that breeds patronage politics can easily engender its demise. Sorauf (1959) concludes: 'As the great day of patronage recedes into history, one is tempted to say that the advancing merit systems will not kill patronage before it withers and dies of its own infirmity and old age' (ibid., p. 34).

The nature of election campaigns also determines the kind of party worker that is attracted to the party, which in turn prefigures the possibility of patronage politics. For those parties whose campaigning emphasises less door-to-door canvassing and mailing, and more national and centralised forms (such as mass media and advertising), there is less reliance on a massive presence of cadreship.

Rather, where person-power is required, parties can rely more on organised bodies such as commercial associations and trade unions, than individuals who expect personal rewards. Organised bodies do so, of course, in expectation of accruing some benefit. Their benefits are channelled through legislation and policies, but without the corrosive effect of inappropriate appointments or tolerance of ineptitude because it provides livelihood.

A welfare state also has the potential to undercut the appeal of parties as providers of patronage. The social welfare function, which was one charitable function that was largely fulfilled by parties, has now been taken over by the welfare state. By and large, welfare services, which one accesses directly from the State, have the potential to innoculate poor people against crass appeals for votes in return for patronage. For the welfare state does provide what would have otherwise been provided by a patron-party (Sorauf, 1959).

In other words, as Bearfield (2009) argues, patrons invoke a variety of 'patronage styles' in pursuit of their principal, or principle goals:

- Organisational patronage is used to strengthen or create political organisations.
- Democratic patronage seeks to achieve democratic or egalitarian goals using patronage.
- Tactical patronage uses the distribution of public office to bridge political or policy goals.
- Reform patronage emerges when those committed to reforming the

existing patronage system themselves engage in the practice as the means of replacing the corrupt political regime that preceded them (Bearfield, 2009, p. 68).

POVERTY AND AFFLUENCE AND HOW THEY ARTICULATE WITH PATRONAGE

Does social mobility reduce the appeal of patronage? As stated earlier, it is not the purpose of this study to assess whether patronage in South Africa manifests more intensely in poor rather than affluent communities. Such juxtaposition would be unhelpful, given that patronage suggests the dispensing of resources of various kinds, thus cutting across considerations of social status. In any case, it would be trite to argue the absence of patronage among the affluent, if their movement to higher social status was, for instance, an outcome of the 'original sin' of patronage.

Some have suggested that, theoretically, the middle-class does not rely on patronage for livelihood. They have the education and skills to secure employment in the private sector without seeking the party to intercede on their behalf. The presence and vibrancy of a private sector is therefore critical in undercutting the saliency of patronage. It offers an alternative source of employment, and makes employment selection independently of political influence. One need not be a political loyalist to secure employment in the private sector, nor can political parties necessarily insist that private companies employ individuals with political connections. Skilled job-seekers are likely to prefer private sector employment over a political appointment in the public sector, for a change of government may lead to termination of service. Skilled people, therefore, are less likely to respond to parties' approaches to vote in return for jobs.

According to this argument, education helps to instil civic mindedness. Educated individuals are often enticed into party work, and do so not in expectation of material rewards, but out of conviction, seeing it as a civic virtue. Civic minded citizens are more independent voters than 'patronage-seeking party-liners, the public spirited citizen rather than the self-interested party worker' (Sorauf, 1960, p. 30).

In other words, education helps create a party cadre that is 'motivated by belief, by loyalty to an attractive candidate, by a sense of civic duty, or by a more generalised social and sporting enthusiasm' and regards 'political activity more as avocation than vocation' (ibid. p. 31).

However, the South African experience includes the reality that historical exclusion and marginalisation of the majority of the population existed alongside – and in fact undergirded – mass patronage to the white community in the form of race-based privileges extended to white workers, the white middle class, and white business. Forcible alienation from land, job reservation, unequal education, restrictions on trading opportunities, apportioning of mineral resources – as well as giving contracts to companies associated with the security establishment – all reflect instances of a system that was founded on racial patronage, and the effects of this live with us in the racial disparities that are the legacy of the colonial system.

In relation to post-apartheid South Africa, account has to be taken of a sizeable segment of educated citizens, and the middle and upper classes who rely on state patronage to occupy senior positions in both the public and private sectors. For these citizens, patronage is a fundamental driver of their privileged status, and their tenuous material position makes them even more dependent on patronage. They become obsessed with material accumulation as a marker of their newly found social status. This builds up into a financial burden, which is increased by the fact that, unlike their white middle-class counterparts, and in addition to their own nuclear families, they have extended families to support. 'As a consequence', according to Joel Netshitenzhe, 'they have to rely on debt and/or patronage. Having dipped their toes into that lifestyle, but with no historical backup, some then try to acquire the resources by hook or by crook' (Netshitenzhe, 2012, p. 2).

MUNICIPALITIES AS A CONTESTED TERRAIN: PATRONAGE, IMMIGRATION AND THEIR MANY FACES IN LOCAL GOVERNANCE

Although migration to South Africa has been a fact of life for more than a century, and African township residents have lived and even intermarried with foreign Africans in the black townships, the past decade has seen a rise in xenophobic attitudes that have increasingly taken violent forms. Media reports and a recent study by Karl von Holdt (2011) have shown how most, if not all, of these violent 'xenophobic' flare-ups have site-specific dynamics. That is, they are embedded within the broader local politics, linked often with the levels of service delivery and internal politics of the ANC local, regional, and sometimes national, role-players. Local government, as the primary experience of the State that communities encounter, is a locus where these fairly new phenomena are playing out: the public's expression of displeasure at poor service delivery, and the increasing scapegoating of the most vulnerable people within poor communities – foreign Africans. Understanding what is happening in the country in this respect becomes imperative.

As South Africa traverses a period of transition, shifts in claims of citizenship spawn fissures within communities that coexisted during the apartheid era (then held together by common experiences of access, or lack of access to public goods, and personal and social mobility). The rapid class formations currently underway are producing what Hanson (von Holdt, 2011) calls 'differentiated citizenship'. This dispensation 'distributes treatment, rights, and privileges differentially among formally equal citizens according to differences of education, property, race, gender, and occupation' (von Holdt, 2011, p. 6–7). It could be cautiously suggested that the 2012 unrest in the platinum (and later gold) mining belt, is indicative of some of the dynamics at play relevant to this notion. In trying to unpack the violent protests that have become a constant feature at the local government level, Von Holdt (2011) is discerning what he calls an 'insurgent citizenship' that is organising itself around claims that 'destabilise the differentiated'.

What is relevant for this study from Van Holdt's report is the growing dexterity of 'subaltern groups' at the narrow local government level, with which legitimate grievances of communities over lack of delivery or lack of responsiveness to their complaints and needs are manipulated to carve patron-client relationships. These struggles over the meaning of citizenship become also struggles over rank, status, and power, a microcosm of the broader contestation over hierarchy, status, and social order within and between elites and subalterns. Thus the key protagonists in these insurgencies play to the needs expressed by those within their sphere of influence. These could play out on the following levels:

- Local traders concerned about the threat of foreign traders within poor communities.
- Communities angered by the lack of service delivery or non-responsive local councillors.
- Political rivalries within local government, or between players at the local and provincial government levels.
- Inter- and intra-party competition over dominance at local government level and the concomitant access to resources to consolidate such dominance.

Von Holdt warns that these insurgencies are not necessarily without sinister motivation. Sometimes they disguise rivalries among the elite, a phenomenon that has the effect of corroding, undermining, and restricting the basis of citizenship (von Holdt, 2011, p. 7).

EXCLUSION ON THE BASIS OF NATIONALITY

In *Nationalism and Ethnicity*, Craig Calhoun (1993) argues that not only are ethnicity and nationalism not receding in modern society, but both are part of a modern set of categorical identities invoked by elites and other participants in political and social struggles.

Neocosmos (2011) demonstrates this when he makes a compelling case that the emerging 'xenophobic discourse' in South Africa is in part a product of the small elite seeking to gain hegemony in the post-apartheid South Africa. Drawing on Franz Fanon's analysis of the emerging nationalist bourgeoisie in post-colonial Africa, *The Wretched of the Earth*, Neocosmos quotes:

> *If the national bourgeoisie goes into competition with the Europeans, the artisans and craftsmen start a fight against non-national Africans... These foreigners are called on to leave; their shops are burned, their street stalls are wrecked, and in fact the government...commands them to go, thus giving their nationals satisfaction* (Neocosmos, 2011, p. 381).

Again, demonstrating Calhoun's contention, Neocosmos makes this claim elsewhere:

> *Given the fact that the new Black elite stress their indigeneity and nativism in order to justify access to rights and resources, the poor follow suit by also stressing nativism in order to acquire what they see as their own entitlements* (Neocosmos, 2011, p. 381).

INTERNATIONAL LESSONS: MEXICO AND KENYA

Mexico and Kenya shed light on the contrasting impact of competitive politics on the saliency of patronage politics.

Mexico, a country with a relatively similar socio-economic profile as South Africa, offers an instructive insight into prospects of overhauling patronage politics. Events in the last 20 years or so have seen a reconfiguration of both government and the party system, especially the old nationalist, revolutionary party, Partido Revolucionorio Institucional (PRI) (Institutional Revolutionary Party).

The PRI was formed in 1929, shortly after the success of the Mexican revolution by individuals who had spearheaded the revolution. It single-handedly dominated Mexican politics for about 70 years, partly helped by patronage politics. Party activists were appointed into positions without regard to merit. The party was particularly popular among the urban poor and peasantry, which served as a 'mass clientele' for the PRI.

The party, Ward (1998) asserts, 'used service provision and land regularisation as the cannon fodder for mobilising its political machine... Scarcity ... heightened the stakes and the opportunities for clientelism, which the PRI exploited to good effect' (Ward, 1998, p. 357–8).

Ward contends that since the 1990s, however, the party has been shifting away from patronage politics towards greater emphasis on technocracy in government. In its recruitment for positions, 'party affiliation or sympathy is no longer a sine qua non for appointment to public office' (ibid., p. 350). There is also a trend to retain staff, rather than having a newly elected official bring in his or her own people upon election. Middle and low level management is retained, and there is a relatively low rate of turnover.

The catalyst for change was the onset of competitive politics and consequent loss of support to opposition parties, especially to the Partido Accion Nacional (PAN) (National Action Party). Half of the country fell under opposition rule after the July 1997 elections. And in 2000 the PRI lost the presidential race to the PAN for the first time. Long years of political dominance had made PRI complacent, performing poorly in government. Voters subsequently became disillusioned with the party. Opposition parties benefited from that disillusionment, especially once the integrity of the electoral process was guaranteed.

The PAN and the Partido de la Revolución Democrática (Party of Democratic Revolution) (PRD) exercised governance differently to the PRI. Their leadership included professionals and business people who brought new ways of managing government, which, in some instances, brought improvements. Opposition successes in government put enormous pressure on the PRI. It was under pressure to earn votes through delivery, especially because voters had alternatives. Public office was no longer just about providing patronage to the party activists, but also using the public purse to improve governance in order to remain in power.

Opposition governance had a demonstrative effect on the PRI. The opposition demonstrated that governance could not only be done differently, but also showed that different innovations could succeed. The PRI emulated some of the innovations transforming the way in which the party had exercised governance. The PRI of today, according to Ward, is a modernising agent. Although the party still exercises a strong influence on government, and the officials have ties to the party, governance is guided by technical rationality. Indeed, the government programme is still directed by the party agenda and philosophy, as should be the case in a democracy, but its implementation is driven by technical considerations.

Yet, the recent history of Kenya casts doubts over the notion that competitive politics necessarily saps the saliency of patronage politics. The recent account by Kenya's former corruption investigator, John Kithongo, narrated by Michela Wrong in the book *It's Our Turn to Eat: The Story of a Kenyan Whistle-Blower* (2009) tells a story of persistent corruption even under conditions of competitive politics. Mwai Kibaki's coalition government, made up of former opposition parties simply continued where its predecessor, Arap Moi's KANU, had left off. Rather than clean up government, Kibaki's government (according to John Kithongo, who was appointed to investigate corruption) resolved that it was now 'their turn to eat', just like their predecessor had done before them.

The varying experiences of the two countries illustrate that competitive politics does not necessarily eradicate patronage politics. Rather, what effect competitive politics has is prefigured by the social context, and the history of a country.

CHAPTER 3

METHODOLOGY

The nature of the subject under study dictated the methodology and sets its own limitation. While researchers may manoeuvre when it comes to selecting research methodologies – on the basis of their experience and what their preferences are, or even field of study within which the subject matter being studied belongs – the space for such a shift is largely confined by the theme being explored. Even more critical and confining is the manner in which the hypothesis or assumptions regarding the subject matter is framed. An open-ended exploratory hypothesis requires that the research methodology employed provides a space for the discovery of the unknown. In cases where the hypothesis or assumptions are not open-ended, then a stricter approach and confining research methodology have to be employed. Such a methodology would confine the researcher to remain disciplined and less exploratory, primarily because the assumptions laden in the hypothesis are much stronger, and consequently should not leave much space for discovery of the unknown.

This study aims to explore the relationship between poverty and patronage politics in South Africa. While other studies have been carried out on near-similar themes to the subject of this report, with the aim to explore how patronage politics has proliferated in post-apartheid South Africa, the point of departure for this study is not to cast a judgement on whether patronage undermines fair and open political engagements. Rather, the study explores how the institutions of patronage are intertwined with poverty, and how that relationship is expressed in institutions, or how it is further institutionalised. The aim is to explore and develop a systematic way of understanding patronage qua institution that mediates relationships in the public space. Poverty is looked at as a specific terrain in which patronage politics gets rooted, and shapes institutions with the study throwing light on the impact that this interrelationship of poverty, inequality, and patronage has on local democracy and life.

In the study, the hypothesis on the relationship between poverty and patronage is deliberately loosely formulated with a clear intention to explore the subject beyond our initial assumptions, or the assumptions that are carried in the literature on the subject. The study aims to outline the typology of patronage, and also to understand the institutional space that comes to be defined as patronage, with the aim to assess the extent poor people experience the prevalence, and even the sustenance, of patronage.

As South Africa's post-apartheid institutions are evolving, there is an institutional gap left behind by the cessation of some apartheid-bound institutions. The 'new' institutions of democracy inaugurated in 1994 would be built against the background of completely collapsed institutions on the one hand, and the carry-over of institutions into the new dispensation on the other. Patronage as an institution in society can be carried over from the old order by way of being reformulated into new institutions. Patronage can also be built afresh into new institutions. In some cases, the formation of new institutions of patronage can express itself in the form of institutional instability. Conversely, the carry-over of old institutions and the reformulation and use of such institutions into patronage institutions may correlate with a period of less social instability than is the case where institutions are completely formed from a zero base.

It is important to note, therefore, that by its nature, patronage cannot simply be identifiable as a stand-alone phenomenon. Patronage may take the form of institutions through which it expresses itself. It is for this reason that the study does not approach patronage as an expression of ailment in the institutions or society, rather it attempts to study how patronage gets embedded in institutions and also the type of social resistance that patronage sparks within communities. In other words, how does patronage become part of institutions in society? As such, to study patronage is also to observe the nature of social resistance that societies would mobilise as a response to patronage. In some areas, it is these types of resistance that give an indication of how patronage is embedded in institutions of power.

In order to fully discern the relationship between poverty and the nature, and even the extent, of patronage, inequality plays an important role. While inequality does not cause poverty, inequality is one of the most notable consequences of poverty. In some areas, on the one hand, poverty may be distributed more equitably across society, and inequality may not necessarily be prevalent. On the other hand, inequality may exist where poverty is not prevalent.

The case of South Africa, however, is not complex when it comes to understanding the relationship between poverty and inequality. There is a strong positive correlation between poverty and inequalities across different communities. This trend is evident at a national aggregate level and also at local government level within communities. Inequality is an indication of the economy's inability to distribute resources and opportunities equitably. The roots of such a problem are multiple, ranging from poor economic growth, which leaves fewer resources for distribution, for example. Poor distribution of resources may equally result from a lack of proper institutions through which distribution may take place. In such a contracted space where the economy's normal distributive channels are not available, or have been disturbed over a period of time, patronage may be resorted to as an instrument of redistribution.

One of the effects of apartheid has been that the system consistently and systematically undermined and destroyed channels of distributing resources among communities, allowing a space for alternative institutions to emerge. Education is a channel through which resources are distributed in society, which the apartheid system completely undermined. Such institutions would not be rebuilt overnight while the need to ensure distribution of resources in society could not be suppressed or suspended. In this scenario, institutions of patronage may emerge to serve this purpose.

Much can be said in relation to the manner in which patronage undermines democratic institutions. This study does not aim to contend this point. The aim of this study, however, is to understand patronage as an institution that emerges in the process of democratic consolidation in South Africa. In that way, we also observe patronage as a competing institution that preys on an empty space that may exist in a particular socio-economic context. Where normal institutions, through which open competition for resources are constricted, patronage may provide opportunities for upward mobility outside the dominant groups (Blanton, Mason, & Athow, 2001). Patronage may be internal to institutions, or may rather be a constant agent to effect changes for those who operate outside dominant institutions.

In order to fully comprehend the relationship between poverty, inequality, and patronage, the hypothesis had to be formulated in a way that leaves more space to fully observe some of the unknown aspects of patronage, particularly how it is perceived by those who are in the space where it is practiced. The nature of the subject explored in this study, as explained, prescribes a snowballing 'ethnographic' appreciation. There are challenges to this methodological approach in the sense that it goes to the conception of the very notion of patronage and may perpetually confine researchers to constant abstraction on the subject instead of testing the research hypothesis. The advantage of this approach, however, is that it allows researchers to contribute towards a deeper and improved understanding of concepts at play, allowing for further reflection on such concepts. It further avoids a one-sided exploration of the negative impact of patronage on societies, and also evinces explorations on how patronage is perceived by communities and therefore what type of resistance, if any, is sparked by these perceptions.

A field survey or ethnographic research method has been thus selected to measure the adequacy of assumptions made on the existence of patronage. The aim in pursuing field surveys is also to capture the history of the sites which provide context to under social behaviour. In *Area Study and Discipline: A Useful Controversy?* Robert Bates argues that certain behaviour can be understood and explained better when observed in context (1997, p. 168). For example, the building of a network of patronage through which resources are distributed could amount to corruption at face value. When understood in the historical context of the collapse of institutions in an area, this behaviour could amount to the process of re-institutionalisation. The historical context, which can be understood through a deep ethnographic study, would help to develop a nuanced understanding of patterns of behaviour such as patronage.

SELECTION OF SITES

In order to fully understand how to gauge patronage, it is necessary to first identify indicators that need to be assessed. The existence of patronage in South Africa, as already alluded to, can be explained with reference to a number of factors. It is important to ask: what are the defining methods of organising societies through which patronage is proliferated? This speaks to how patronage practices actually take place. Are there peculiar features such as cultural or religious traits through which patronage relations are proliferated? This refers not to factors that cause patronage, but factors that serve as channels or conduits for organising patron-client relations. Those factors would, under certain circumstances, exist even where patronage is not observable.

What are the underlying causes of patronage or conditions in which it takes root? These speak to causes of patronage or conditions which favour it in society, not the peculiar manner in which patronage is proliferated (referred to above). If we take it that patronage could be aggravated or encouraged by poverty, the explanatory power of poverty as a factor that enables particular forms of patronage should be scientifically observable. Factors that cause patronage should rather have similar effect on patronage, irrespective of the cultural or more peculiar traits in society. The lower level of democratisation – which should give indication to a particular set of indicators – may be thought about as one of the causes of relations of patronage, for example. The levels of democratisation are also indicative of the levels of institutionalisation in society. It is important to note, however, that democratic institution does not solely define relations in society.

It has been argued that patronage is not necessarily less predominant in a competitive party system. This shows, therefore, that political competition measured in terms of openness of the political system is not a strong explanatory variable when it comes to understanding why patronage exists. A competitive party system is rather a *dependent* variable, whose fusion with an independent variable may explain the levels of patronage in society. There is a relationship between poverty, ethnic competition, and patronage. The task – which begins with the selection of cases for observation – is to engage in a deeper enquiry that would seek to understand the manifestation of that relationship.

The cases selected for observation in this study reflect local government demarcation. The following quote by Robert Bates, in *Modernization, Ethnic Competition, and the Rationality of Politics in Contemporary Africa* (1973), demonstrates fully how local government is a scene for the propagation of patronage:

> *Given that power over the distribution of many of the benefits of modernity is vested in the local administration, and given the correspondence between administrative and ethnic boundaries, it is natural that persons would create politically cohesive groups and utilize these to restrict the degree to which the administration could compel the sharing of benefits with others. The demand of ethnic groups for their own districts and council represents a logical continuation of this process, for by securing this demand they could more perfectly exclude others*

from such benefits and thereby reserve to themselves a larger portion (Bates: 1997, p. 158).

It is within this context that patronage needs to be explored at the local government level in South Africa. Local government offers the necessary level of proximity to institutions of power and the apparition of power. It is institutions of power that are responsible for distribution of resources and opportunities. Patronage emerges in relation to the institutions of power, either by way of complementing them, or competing with them in the process of distribution of resources. Competition for resources is quite intense at local government level, and it is mediated by various social, cultural, religious, and political traits. To effectively measure how patronage is mediated, different indicators should be observed in each case at local government level. The selection of units of analysis is quite crucial, and some of those units would be more prevalent on one site than in others. Our selection of sites for observation is sensitive to such variations.

In selecting the sites, it is important to bear in mind the need not only to explain patronage where it exists at local government level, but also to explain the *absence* of patronage where it does not exist, despite conditions for its existence prevailing. This is possible through the selection of cases where varied configuration of indicators is observable. It is the relational structure of indicators that is crucial. A great deal of assumptions have been proposed regarding what, when it comes to explaining patronage, are the independent variables. This study does not venture into finding answers to that question. Rather, it examines the manifestations of patronage under conditions in which poverty is rife. The areas we selected for observation are characterised by this dynamic. At the same time, they differed in certain respects: for example in their access to economic opportunities, or natural resources, or in being more or less socially homogenous, and so on.

SITES FOR OBSERVATION

The study has been carried out across four provinces in South Africa, namely Western Cape, Gauteng, Free State, and Eastern Cape. Different sites demarcated along municipal wards were selected in those respective provinces. The following map represents areas that have been studied within the provinces. The localities that have been selected indicate variance in terms of their history, institutional culture, and also political tradition. This variance, as it will be shown in our findings, plays a significant role in testing the strengths of explanations of patronage, and how they manifest themselves.

Figure 1: Map of South Africa reflecting provinces

Province	Municipality	Area & Ward no
Gauteng	City of Johannesburg	– Diepsloot (ward 95, 113)
Free State	1. Nketoana 2. Maluti-a-Phofung	– Reitz/Petsana (ward 8, 9) – Phuthaditjaba; – Monontsha
Eastern Cape	Mhlontlo Municipality	– Qumbu – Tsolo
Western Cape	Overstrand Municipality	– Kleinmond (ward 9) – Hangklip (ward 10) – Greater Hermanus (ward 5) – Gansbaai Stanford (ward 6) – Buffeljachts (ward 11)

Table 1: Sites Selected For Observation

The sites that have been selected for observation have both similarities and differences. They also posed different challenges when it came to gaining entry and securing interviews with role players and community members residing in the areas. As part of ethnographic enquiry, the challenges confronted in the sites were captured so as to help elucidate the context against which interviews were conducted and the information was attained. The local government environment in South Africa has its own peculiarities, predominated by the tension that exists in relation to delivery of services and concerns harboured by communities. Being the most immediate form of government, and the expression of governance for the majority of citizens, local government structures are difficult to gain entry.

Where entry has been relatively easy to attain, community members at times tend to distort the reality on the ground with a clear intention to gain attention from researchers. Spending a prolonged time on the sites reveals that the more available community members are for interviews by outsiders or researchers, the more the probability of the distortion of the reality. In some areas, communities have had an experience of 'research fatigue'. Areas such as Diepsloot in Gauteng, among sites selected for observation, have been researched over and over, and this poses a challenge where interviewees may tend to provide 'template' responses. The research team took a note of this and it was largely resolved through repeated visits to the same place and also repeated interviews of the same people.

Unlike the functioning of national government, which continues to receive attention from the media and researchers, the local government environment does not appear interesting to the media or researchers to attract deeper research interests. The attention deficit experienced at local government level may drive communities to desperate measures where they exaggerate information about their areas with the aims of capturing the interest of researchers, and of making it onto news headlines. The disproportionate spread of attention among different spheres of government has a more direct impact for semi-rural municipalities located on the peripheries.

Our selection of cases for observation shows this disproportionate distribution of attention across different municipalities, which also coincides with the geographical location of municipalities. The political significance of municipalities also suggests the level of media attention that the municipality would attract, subsequently affecting the expression of social tension in the municipalities, and affecting the nature, depth, and representation of information by community members interviewed in the area. In order to fully comprehend what strikes divisions within the areas being observed, it is necessary to provide a brief social, economic, and political sketch of each of the areas. This exercise also provides an indication as to the institutional makeup of the area, therefore shaping the community's responses to patronage, for example.

GAUTENG: DIEPSLOOT

Diepsloot is located in the north of Johannesburg, serving almost as a border between Tshwane and Johannesburg. A densely populated settlement characterised by poverty and high unemployment, Diepsloot is considered one of the newest settlement areas in Gauteng in the sense that it has transited from being an informal settlement to a formal settlement that boasts one of the highest infrastructure outlays in Johannesburg. It was established in 1995 as a transit camp for people who had been removed from Zevenfontein. Potential for growth, and plans for the infusion of developmental projects into Diepsloot, add an important variable in exploring the manifestation of patronage in poverty-stricken communities and its potential impact on delivery of services at the local government level. Joburg City's Spatial Development Framework for 2007/8 for this region estimated that 74% of the housing units in Diepsloot were informal structures.

What makes Diepsloot even more interesting to explore – indeed its suitability as a case study to contribute to our understanding of how communities compete for limited resources – is that being a new settlement area it belongs to no one! Diepsloot carries no 'institutional baggage', and is rather an expression of formulation of social institutions, and, as such, is an excellent case to explore how patronage gets infused in institutions of power from the formative stage, or rather how patronage may emerge where institutions of power are in their infancy and not yet strong enough to repel such a trend. Diepsloot is also a volatile community, having been one of the theatres for the brutal mob killings that came to be known as xenophobic attacks. The population figure in Diepsloot is estimated between 150 000 and 200 000, located in a 5.18 square kilometre area. The main source of economic activity within Diepsloot is trading and informal trading.

WESTERN CAPE: OVERSTRAND MUNICIPALITY

The municipal area of Overstrand covers a surface of almost 1,708 square kilometres. The area has a permanent population of approximately 90 000. The ANC governed the municipality from 1994 until the DA won control in 2002. The areas selected for observation in the Overstrand municipality are better characterised as fishing and agricultural communities. Fishing does not only define their livelihoods, it serves as an arena for social relations for the communities. Overstrand is a coastal rural municipality. Besides fishing, Overstrand also casts itself as a compelling tourist destination, and this is a strong commercial lobbying issue for the municipality. The tourism industry depends on the patronage of local tourists, particularly visitors from Gauteng province.

Being dependent on a formal sector such as fishing, and also tourism, Overstrand notably has a rich culture of forums through which communities organise themselves to tackle the economic difficulties they confront, particularly to strive towards inclusion in the fishing industry. The formality of the nature of economic opportunities in Overstrand is such that it promotes a more formal response through forums such as civil society organisations, commerce and investors' forums, fishermen's and fisherwomen's forums, and faith based organisations, for example. The main source of economic activity in the area is dependent on natural resources, primarily fishing and tourism.

EASTERN CAPE: MHLONTLO MUNICIPALITY

Mhlontlo municipality falls under the OR Tambo district municipality in the Eastern Cape. Some 67% of the total population of Mhlontlo municipality reside in rural (traditional) dwellings, with 29% in formal dwellings and 3% in informal dwellings. Ward 19 (the sample area) is in the Hlubi traditional authority with nine administrative areas. The municipality is under strong ANC control. The ANC has won 96% of votes, with the African People's Convention, Civic Independent, and the Democratic Alliance attaining less than 1%, and the Congress of the People and the United Democratic Movement, 1.5% and 2.5% respectively.

Free State: Nketoana municipality and Maluti-a-Phofung

Maluti-a-Phofung is a large municipality covering most of the area around Phuthaditjaba. Nketoana municipality, on the other hand, is a fairly small municipality with nine wards. These municipalities find themselves in the Free State, one of the poorer provinces in South Africa. Unemployment in the Free State is high. Maluti-a-Phofung municipality is a semi-urban environment with rural areas as close as 10 kilometres from the regional centre, while Nketoana comprises townships and newly emerging settlements on the outskirts of Reitz. The more semi-urban status of QwaQwa is a throwback to the apartheid homeland system under the Mopeli dynasty. As a result, QwaQwa boasts more superior infrastructure such as stadiums, decent schools, and also strikingly modern structures that house municipal offices. These are, of course, inherited from the homeland system.

Beyond the infrastructure, QwaQwa seems to have a sense of order, while Nketoana does not. The institutional makeup of QwaQwa is completely different from that of Nketoana, which is a more volatile municipality with higher numbers of social protests.

The diversity of institutional mechanism across the sites

Each and every site that has been selected for sampling has a distinct institutional culture. The specific nature of institutions identified in all the sites has an impact on the manner in which the respective communities respond to the challenge of poverty and inequality. The diversity in the institutional culture of the sites allows for us to test the adequacy of emerging explanations on the causes and manifestations of patronage. For example, Mhlontlo municipality has a history of traditional authority, which poses a challenge, but also an opportunity to measure the prevalence, or lack, of patronage. Traditional authorities may usurp civil society formation as the institution becomes the supra-authority, embodying both governance and civic culture.

In a situation where old traditional authorities are more prevalent, opportunities for the emergence of other forms of institutions are limited. As such, the 'old' institutions become a channel for the expression and dispensing of patronage. This may also limit competition for resources, as it is through institutions such as these – civil society formations – that individuals and groups compete for resources. A similar trend is also observable in the case of QwaQwa, where there is a strong prevalence of traditional authority. The effect of traditional institutions in QwaQwa – particularly the manner in which the institutions close the space for emerging competing institutions – is comparable to the experience in Mhlontlo. In other words, where traditional leadership institutions are prevalent, the social discontent sparked by patronage, or any ills in the locality, is not openly expressed. And furthermore, political party contests may be subjected to old institutions.

Areas such as Diepsloot and Nketoana municipality, also observed in the study, have had no sustained period of institutional stability since 1994. These are areas where the post-apartheid dispensation has seen the formation of new institutions altogether: institutions that were formed in emergent municipalities. In this setting, competition for resources and opportunities has been rife and there are many institutions that are used as channels for such competition. In this area, the perception about patronage would most likely be stronger than would be the case with closed institutions (such as those experienced under traditional authorities). The more there are institutional channels for competition for resources, the stronger the perception that patronage exists.

The areas that are observed in this study vary in terms of the institutional mechanisms in place, and the nature of economic activities predominant in each area. For the case of the Overstrand municipality, the area is predominantly in pursuit of a 'moral economy', where agriculture, tourism, and fishing are the most dominant drivers. This feature underlies the social base for the manner in which the community would organise itself to negotiate ways to play a role in the economy. According to Munro, '...the moral economy underwrites locally understood concepts of rights, property rights, and community membership, which make agrarian communities resilient in the face of environmental or political stress' (Munro, 1996, p. 115). The basis for social mobilisation in Overstrand municipality has to do with the distribution of fishing rights and how that impacts upon environmental conservation in the area. While Overstrand is not generally known for its rebellious activities, the community lobbying of the formal structure through which economic rights are being transferred to communities (in the form of fishing rights, for example) is attempted through formal structures such as NGOs. The space within which the lobbying for a more equitable distribution of economic right takes place would also be affected and might also give rise to further proliferation of patronage.

Units of Analysis

Competition for limited resources can take place along racial, ethnic, and also class lines. While class has not attracted much attention when it comes to analysing economic competition in South Africa (or Africa for that matter), there are strong indications that class underwrites conflict even in areas where ethnicity or race have been dominant factors in the past. This study does not concern itself with the question of whether it is class, race, or ethnicity that defines the proliferation of patronage in South Africa. What matters the most here, is that social mobilisation that may be represented in the form of patronage is usually targeted at influencing how the state distributes resources and opportunities.

Emmanuel Wallerstein states that:

> ...while groups' social activities are in some ultimate sense determined by their role in the world economy, the objective of their political activity (to secure or transform their position in the social system) is ordinarily directed as the state of which they are a member ('citizen') (Wallerstein, 1973, p. 377).

The 'practical utility' (Ake, 1993, p. 244) of any available social base is identified by communities who seek to further their goals. The elites will always make efforts to define units of activities within communities. Class or ethnicity might be accentuated by the elites at any point in time as part of the political project. However, there are limitations as to the extent to which the elites would influence the social base: 'Although the elite have an exceptionally high profile in the African democracy movement, and largely dominate its leadership, they do not constitute its social base' (Ake, 1993, p. 240).

The sites that are selected for observation also have a varying institutional legacy and that has an impact on the existence of rebellious activities in the respective area. The institutional legacy is a determinant of the presence, intensity, and frequency of rebellious activities. At the centre of the conflict lies a struggle for resources and mobilisation of such struggles across different communities. This frequency does not always explain the existence of patronage, but rather the perception of patronage, which serves as a point of mobilisation for rebellious activities.

Conversely, in communities where the institutional mechanisms have had less disruption, thus where post-apartheid institutions have had less impact on the institutional mechanism, mobilisation of rebellious activities is quite low and evidence may point to proliferation of patronage along traditional lines. In such cases as QwaQwa, for example, the new institution of local government has been less disruptive of the 'old' traditional institutions. The fusion of the new institutions into the old ones, and the mobilisation of civil society in a way that does not disrupt the institutional mechanism, has resulted in tranquillity, while patronage is underway as part of the new system.

The level of resistance against politics of patronage – expressed either in the form of internal party lobbying or mobilisation of rebellious activities such as social protest – does not have a direct link with the actual instances of patronage. A deeper explanation of the disjuncture is also sought in the study.

ACCESS TO INTERVIEWEES AND GAINING TRUST

In the entire fieldwork experience, gaining access to people for interview has not been difficult when it comes to individual community members or lobby groups such as NGOs. In most cases, difficulty arose in gaining access to local government officials and to some extent councillors. Our field survey could not stray off the usual trust issue at local government level. Due to lack of trust, it has been difficult for communities to gain access to local government information and to officials. In some cases, even access to information such as IDPs, which should be publicly available in any case, was not easy to obtain.

Interviewees' availability to participate in interviews was also driven by self-interest in the sense that most intended to inform outsiders about their local conditions, so their issues could be propelled to national importance. This motive of course has tended to result in exaggeration of information and omission of certain information while emphasis is made to drive the local agenda.

Councillors who were interviewed also attempted to influence the researcher's decision as to who else to interview. This manoeuvre reflects the nature and character of local politics and the inherent competition in the management of the flow of information.

Trust is generally low at local government level, and more so when outsiders are involved in seeking information. To get residents' co-operation, researchers undertook not to use their real names. This is also a security measure, to protect them against possible victimisation. In the instance of public officials, however, we have used their real names.

ETHICAL CONSIDERATION

Negotiating entry into the field also posed an ethical challenge. In some cases, communities gave entry on the pretext that their concerns would be reported in the media. While it might be necessary for researchers to level with interviewees and state that the information collected will only be used for the purpose of research, and not to expose community concerns in the media, at times this perception as held by the community could only be corrected in subsequent visits. The communities' understanding of the nature and purpose of this research developed gradually with further visits.

CHAPTER 4

RESEARCH FINDINGS

This chapter presents the research findings from the case studies. It draws largely from individual and group interviews, as well as from focus group interviews from all five sites. Some of the insights are informed by observations researchers made in the course of fieldwork. Socio-economic data, from Statistics South Africa, is cited to provide further context and meaning.

The findings shed light on the relationship between poverty and inequality on the one hand, and patronage-politics on the other. The focus on poverty does not preclude an examination of the interaction between the affluent, and local politicians. As such, the findings below begin with a socio-economic profile of our case studies. This provides a useful background and context within which the research questions of this study play out. Thereafter, we look at how residents make their living. This includes survival strategies that the indigent and unemployed poor use in order to eke out a living and the tension that ensues from competition for resources.

Our findings also speak to whether or not the State is providing sufficient assistance to local initiatives towards economic activity. Official assistance is then examined within a broader theme of the presence (or absence) of the State in local communities. Finally, the chapter presents findings on rivalry among the local political elite and the impact thereof on governance, and the conduct of politics in general.

All these themes are fundamental in understanding not only how the various forms of patronage manifest themselves, but also the conditions under which patronage thrives.

ECONOMIC STRUCTURE AND EMPLOYMENT PROFILE

As noted in the preceding chapter, our case study populations are largely poverty-stricken and suffer from relatively high unemployment rates. These problems are especially salient in the semi-rural and former bantustan townships of Nketoana, Maluti-a-Phofung and in the villages of Mhlontlo, as well as in Diepsloot. These lack viable economic activity.

Located in the former Transkei, for instance, Mhlontlo is indicative of the labour supplier status which the former bantustan assumed within the broader South African economy. The Transkei region had the highest number of The Employment Bureau of Africa (Teba) offices, which recruited migrant labourers for the mining industry. Most of the Teba offices were concentrated in the nearby town of Lusikisiki. Families were left headed largely by women, dependent on (sometimes irregular) remittances sent by their migrant-labour spouses.

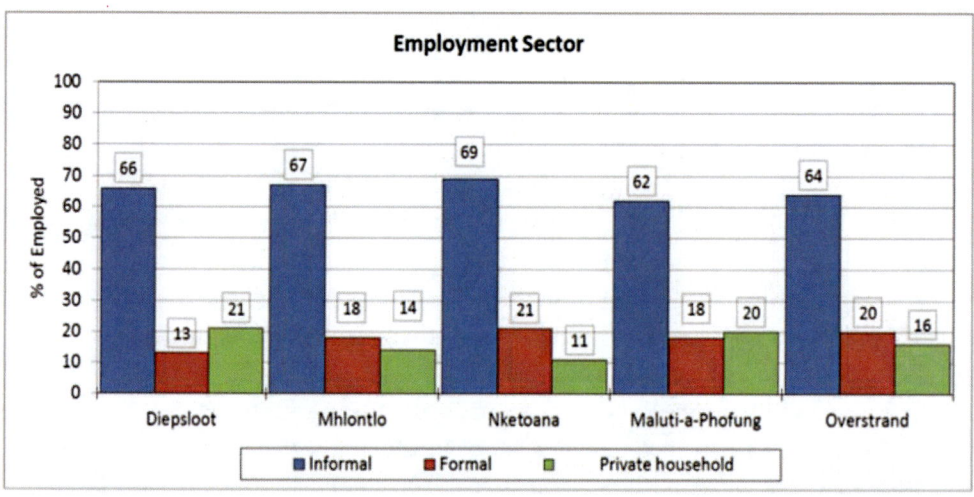

Figure 2: Employment Sector, Source: Census 2011: Community Profiles in SuperCross, published by Stats SA

Local formal employment, therefore, is largely offered by the State. This pertains also to Nketoana and Maluti-a-Phofung, both of which are located in rural towns and in the former QwaQwa bantustan. The agricultural sector in these areas has been hard hit in the last few years, leading to the shedding of jobs. The State is the major employer of municipal labourers, teachers, and clerks. Only a sprinkling of the retail industry constitutes the little there is of the private sector. Cessation of production on some farms has also resulted in migration towards Nketoana, especially in search of employment and residence. The new arrivals are adding to the burgeoning population of shanty and backyard dwellers.

Though characterised by unemployment, these communities do not suffer a total lack of economic opportunity. Mhlontlo's rural villages have access to communal agricultural land and Overstrand's residents to the ocean. Overstrand is a coastal area, offering a range of activities from fishing and eco-tourism to agriculture. The active harbour of Kleinmond is a hive of fishers' activity. It is the industrial hub for commercial abalone (perlemoen) and development of further aquaculture farms is anticipated. Winemaking is the major agricultural activity. Wine farms are a prominent feature of Overstrand's landscape.

The area's natural beauty and diverse animal life are major tourist attractions. For instance, there is a thin belt between the mountains and the Atlantic Ocean that hosts high peaks and fynbos-covered mountain slopes, rivers and streams tumbling over edges to pristine beaches. There is also a wide variety of animals, birds, and insects living in the indigenous forest and fine bush (www.maxabella.co.za). The coastal zone up to Hermanus features several Blue Flag status beaches with several lagoons, wonderful hikes, walks, and various hospitality establishments. It is also known as the best land-based whale-watching destination in South Africa. Among the attractions offered by the ocean is shark cage diving, which has become synonymous with Gansbaai. Specialised boats leave from the Kleinbaai harbour daily for extreme adventure seekers to have close encounters with Great White sharks.

Availability of resources, however, does not imply that they are accessible. Whether residents take advantage of the natural endowment depends on other factors. One such factor is personal means and facilities. Overstrand's population is starkly unequal, which has meant that some exploit the natural endowment more than others. State intervention is also critical in enabling access and providing tangible support.

And because these communities are particularly poor, the State assumes an even greater role in their lives. It provides a livelihood in the form of both grants and employment. This puts those in control of the State, such as councillors, in a significantly influential position. Locals become indebted and vulnerable to councillors. Their role is demanded even more in informal settlements, such as Diepsloot, where services are desperately needed and there is social tension.

Diepsloot sprang up as an informal settlement. The shanty township offered relatively easy informal residence to migrants and immigrants from rural South Africa, the continent, and from other countries as far afield as Pakistan and Bangladesh. Equally enticing about Diepsloot is that it dangles prospects of employment. This accounts for the youthful and unskilled profile of its largely migrant population.

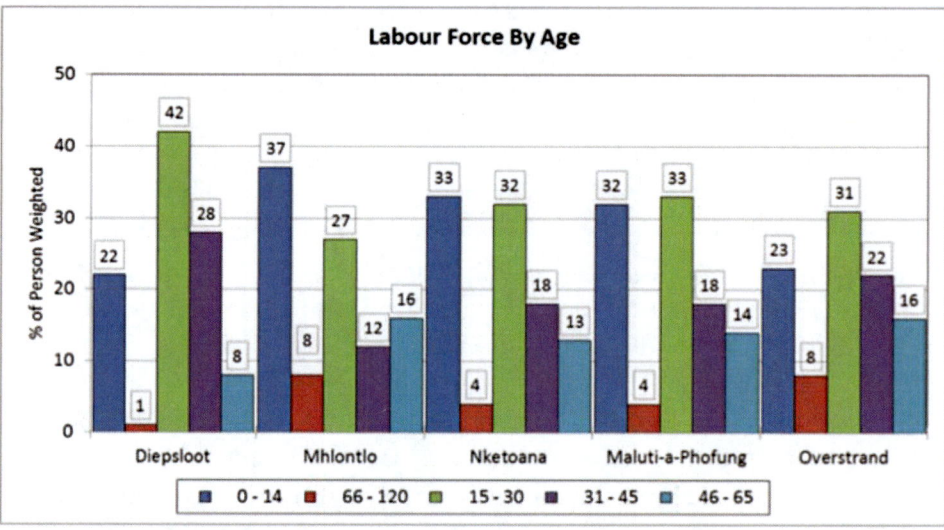

Figure 3: Labour Force by Age
Source: Census 2011: Community Profiles in SuperCross, published by Stats SA

Poverty and unemployment are defining features of Nketoana and Maluti-a-Phofung, Mhlontlo and Diepsloot, whilst it is less pronounced in Overstrand. The latter's relative natural endowment provides locals with opportunities for economic activity. Whether one is able to take advantage of such endowments, however, still depends on access to them. When dire lack of employment forces locals to devise survival strategies and to look elsewhere for subsistence, relative abundance of natural resources posed challenges of access. Who can access the resources and how?

A socio-economic profile that follows provides an insight into people's ways of living, and most importantly, their social status gives an indication on their predisposition towards reliance upon the State and the likelihood of the form in which that State assistance will assume. Dependence induces vulnerability that can be manipulated for other ends, as is shown further below.

MEANS OF LIVELIHOOD AND SCRAMBLE FOR JOBS

In all of the localities, residents rely largely on social wage, whilst some have had to think of ways to eke out a living. The few jobs available elicit intense competition among residents. The intensity of the competition has, in turn, engendered tension among residents.

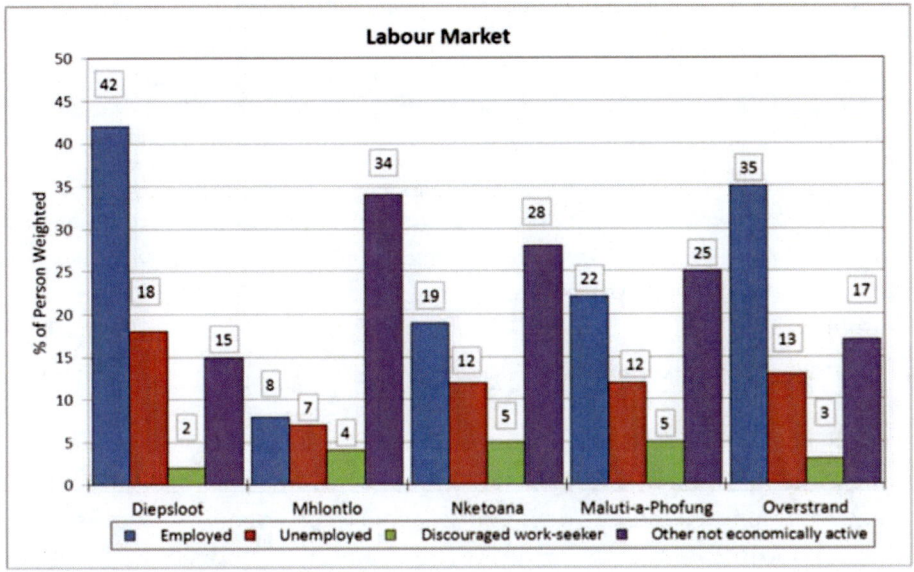

Figure 4: Labour Market, Source: Census 2011: Community Profile in SuperCross, published by Stats SA

Social Assistance

Social grants and employment in the public works programme are the most common forms of social assistance. Relating a problem in Grabouw nearby, but typical of the other four sites as well, Oliphant September – a member of the ANC Regional Executive Committee – put it thus: 'Our people only survive on SASSA grants and the Michael Jackson (child support) grant' (Fieldwork notes: May 25, June 30 2012).

Providing day-to-day living amenities is the one area for which residents are most grateful to the State. It even compensates somewhat for the slow pace of infrastructural development. One resident in Mhlontlo put it thus:

We do not have toilets and we see them in other villages as we pass through the roads and what we can appreciate is the paraffin that SASSA

is giving us; we are happy with the government on that one. People do get the paraffin but the issue of food parcels is going at a snail's pace (Focus group interviews: 7–8 December 2012).

Another resident not only echoed similar sentiments, but also singled out the South African Social Security Agency (SASSA), which falls under the Department of Social Development and Welfare, as a model that other departments should emulate:

I would like to appreciate the work that SASSA does because they say people must not go to town to apply for grants; each and every month they come to us to get people to apply for old-age and child support grants. I wish Home Affairs could do the same and help people with getting IDs because people do not have money to go to town. And when they do go, they find long queues and miss buses going back home. We like what SASSA is doing and so we wish Home Affairs can also do the same (Focus group interviews: 7–8 December 2012).

In other words, even though services may be available, accessing them is oftentimes a problem, especially for low-income and unemployed people. Like Mhlontlo, Hermanus does not have a Home Affairs office to secure critical documents such as birth certificates and identity documents. These documents are critical, especially for indigent people, in accessing social grants. Instead of a permanent office, a mobile office comes 'now and then' to process applications and deliver documents. Though convenient, this service is not easy to secure. One resident explained:

You have to leave your home around eleven, twelve at night, sleep there to be among the first ones when they come … they come in late morning, round about nine. The thing is, you have to be there very early because they will deal with the first ones in line and if you are towards the middle or the end of the line, you are not going to be seen, and that means you are going to go back home (Focus group interviews: 13–14 December 2012).

In Hermanus, if applicants miss the mobile service then they have to go to Caledon. This is the nearest town with a permanent Home Affairs office. And getting there is costly. Residents use public transportation. The total fee, according to one resident, is about R400. For an indigent person that is an astronomical amount. Likewise, Diepsloot residents complain that accessing state opportunities requires spending money they do not have. 'The Department of Labour,' one resident tells us, 'collects information to hire people for internships and learnerships…the nearest labour department here is in Randburg or Midrand.' The problem, though, is that 'if you don't have the R13 for taxi fare to give to the child to go to Midrand to go register for such services, where is that child going to get that kind of information?' (Focus group interviews: 24–25 November 2012).

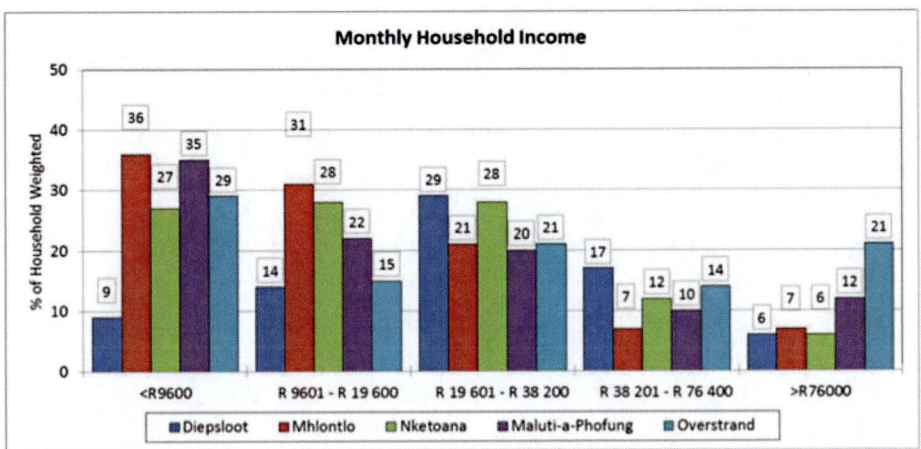

Figure 5: Monthly Household Income Levels, Source: Census 2011: Community Profiles in SuperCross, published by Stats SA

State assistance, however, goes beyond welfare grants to employment. This includes community development workers (CDW) and internships. Though not salaried positions, internships are similarly coveted as they sometimes lead to full employment.

Take Diepsloot's Dolly Motshwane, for instance, who started off as a volunteer in the councillor's office. After three years working as a volunteer she was given a post as a community development worker. Her job entails hearing complaints from individuals within the community and referring them to the relevant government departments. 'My work,' she explained, 'is that of a liaison officer for the community. We are the eyes and ears of government.' (Fieldwork notes: January – February 2012).

Dolly's biography is typical of most residents in Diepsloot. She settled there in 2000 as part of a group that had been trickling in from Skotiphola (an illegally occupied area in the vicinity of northern Johannesburg), fleeing the clashes between the IFP and the ANC. When her husband died she looked and found work as a domestic worker in Victory Park. She then worked for a cleaning company in Houghton, and promptly moved to Hillbrow to get close to her work. But Dolly soon returned to Diepsloot, having concluded that Hillbrow was an unsuitable place for her.

Because it is one of few opportunities available for employment, CDW placements are highly contested by locals. Appointment of one in Mhlontlo, for instance, was frustrated by infighting among two contending factions in the municipality. Each supported a different candidate. A general meeting of Ward 19 in May 2012 provides illuminating details on the impasse. It emerged at the meeting that, at the inception of the initiative back in 2005, appointment of CDWs was largely decided by a ward meeting. This primarily involved ward residents. That is how the initial CDW, Wezile Mhlobo, was appointed. Her subsequent relocation to Mthatha necessitated a replacement. This time round, however, councillors insisted on being involved in the process to decide on the replacement (Fieldwork notes: 22–31 May 2012).

But councillors could not agree on a suitable candidate. Some locals complained that councillors sought to 'parachute an "outsider" to replace Mhlobo', a move highly resisted by locals. Just a week before the Ward 19 meeting, Lulama Ndlabhu was finally appointed CDW, an act some perceived as an 'imposition'. His name, however, was not reflected on the municipality's list of CDWs per ward. Rather, one Handsome Yongama Guqa wass named as a CDW for Ward 19. Repeated telephone calls to Ndlabhu, on a number listed next to his name to verify his appointment went unanswered.

Scramble for Jobs

Severity of unemployment creates intense competition among job seekers for the few available state created jobs. The competition is both among locals, and between locals and foreign-born residents. The result has been tension, which in some instances has exploded into violence.

Asked to describe the job situation at Diepsloot, one informant summed it up as follows:

Jobs are scarce here. As a man you have to get up and do it for yourself (kumele uvuk'u zenzele). You'll see people standing by the roadside as early as 5 o'clock in the morning, waiting to be picked up by umlungu *(white employer). But these* abelungu *don't like us; they prefer these ones from outside.* (Fieldwork notes: October 2011).

In other words, according to our respondent, the most common jobs available are 'painting, working in construction sites, doing gardening work and so on. Those with bricklaying or welding skills tend to get regular call-ups and earn better than unskilled workers' (Fieldwork notes: 22 July 2012). But prospects of employment, even in menial work, as locals complain, are made dim by stiff competition for such work from foreign nationals.

Kleinmond's Oscar Seswane and Olivier Klate, both employees of the Grail Centre Trust – a community development programme – reiterated similar sentiments. Oscar, who has been living in the area since 2000, complained for instance that a newly built SASOL filling station in the neighbourhood only employed foreign nationals without proper working permits in managerial positions, whilst locals remained pump attendants. Oscar went on to add that all local (black) domestic workers are being replaced with foreign nationals. His wife's former employer, Oscar asserts, told her: 'I can get two for the price of one and they won't take me to the CCMA'. As a result, employment for South African domestic workers, according to Oscar, is at its worst level since he moved to Kleinmond 11 years ago (Fieldwork notes: 22 March – 13 April 2012).

A foreign-born resident in Diepsloot pointed out, however, that their advantage over South Africans has less to do with their low wage demands. Rather, they are relatively more skilled than their local counterparts. Most tend to be skilled in carpentry, welding, bricklaying, and electrical work. Such skills are in great demand, making foreign nationals more attractive to prospective employers relative to South Africans (Fieldwork notes: 11 July 2012).

Moreover, the interviewee elaborated that locals are their own worst enemy. 'You see, my brother,' he explained:

South Africans, they like a nice life. They like to buy nice cars and nice clothes. So when they get some money, instead of putting it away to build a business or for their education, they spend the money on nice things. Also, foreigners, they don't need to spend most of their money, they can take a small pay because their living cost is lower than a South African (ibid.).

That said, foreigners are not having it easy, either. Lack of an identification document is a major hindrance to employment. 'That thing', remarked one foreign national, 'causes a problem for me because I can't get a job anywhere'. Even in instances where a prospective employer overlooks their lack of an ID and gives them a job, they still encounter a problem. 'When we get piece jobs', one explained, 'they promise to pay after one week after completing the job. When you go to collect they call the police and when the police come we run away. Yes, we run away and we end up not getting the money from them.'(Focus group interviews: 24–25 November 2012). It is mostly when they are subcontracted, especially by (naturalised) Mozambicans or local whites, that foreign nationals do not experience problems and this tends to be in construction. And they insist on cash payment as they do not have bank accounts due to lack of IDs. Some have tried using another person's account, but get cheated: 'When the money is deposited into the account the account holder would say the money is not in yet' (ibid.).

Feeling outcompeted by foreign nationals, the locals in Diepsloot have, in turn, resorted to organisational mobilisation. In 1999 they formed the Local Development Forum (LDF), whose mission was to fight against unfair allocation of jobs in Diepsloot and 'to shield the Council from taking part in the allocation of jobs in Diepsloot'. The forum had decided that the main criteria for job allocation would be South African citizenship. It set up a labour desk consisting of labour recruitment officers (LROs) who served in a voluntary capacity. The LROs also negotiated rates to circumvent the undercutting of wages by foreigners and curtail competition among desperate job seekers which could potentially undermine their wages. When asked if gender parity was a factor in the LRO criteria, LDF's secretary said they often made sure that women got jobs where they had requisite skills. 'For instance, we would insist that the employers employ women for painting jobs and in cleaning jobs,' he explained (Fieldwork notes: 11 July 2012).

The LDF was ostensibly apolitical. Its leadership was drawn from various backgrounds: representatives of the religious community, non-governmental organisations, the South African Narcotics Association (SANCA), Vuselela, ANCYL, Women's Forum, SANCO, Metro Police, and other political parties such as the National Freedom Party, the Democratic Alliance, and the ANC. 'We were careful not to make this a political thing,' said Mzolisi. The local ANC was represented by its chairman, Chris Vondo, and other prominent ANC members such as Mzolisi Mbikwana, Lefa Nkala, Rogers Makhubela, and then councillor Isaac Maile. Twelve years later, it does not seem as if the

LDF succeeded in remaining apolitical. One resident reported that it had become a subject of control by the various parties and groups.

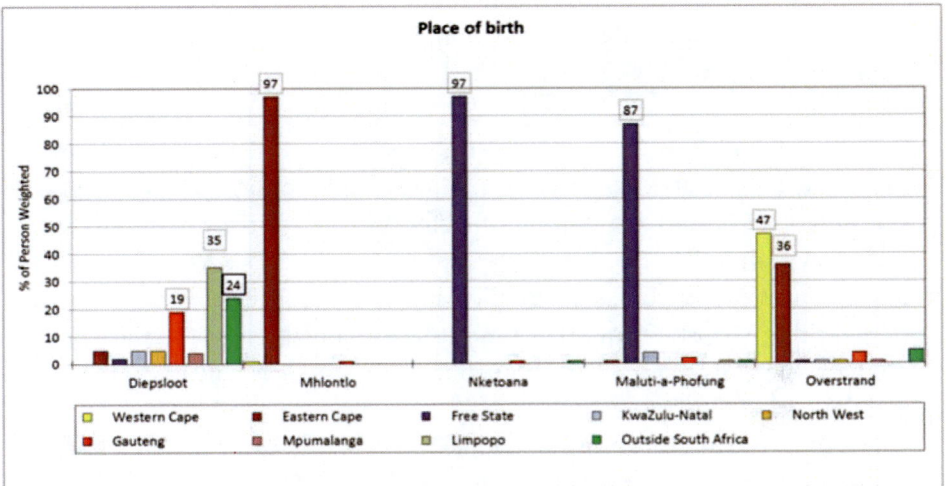

Figure 6: Place of Birth, Source: Census 2011: Community Profiles in SuperCross, published by Stats SA

Albeit the LDF was formed to secure jobs for locals against foreign nationals, the competition for employment was similarly intense among locals. The tag 'outsider' is not only used in reference to foreign nationals, but is also applied to locals who reside elsewhere, yet are employed in the neighbourhood. Locals in Diepsloot expressed frustration that when some jobs become available, people from other townships such as Soweto and Alexandra are bussed in. One respondent pointed out that 'when the Diepsloot Mall was being built, most people working there were not locals, they were bussed in from Soweto' (Interview: October 2011).

Another resident echoed the complaint, and provided an additional example of her own:

What I wanted to say was, especially here in Diepsloot, there are a lot of job opportunities, but we as the residents of Diepsloot do not get them. You find that, for instance here at Lesedi, Diepsloot residents should be able to work there. Diepsloot residents are unemployed, but you find a person from Pretoria working here, or from Alexander working here, but we as residents are sitting unemployed.

And these disabled children are ours; we would like to have a hand in helping them, but people from elsewhere are the ones who have a hand here and all that. Maybe it's the junk, the sweet stuff that are edible that they don't want us to have, but should be given the outsiders. They should mix. Diepsloot is our residential area, and we also want to work in it (Focus group interviews: 24–25 November 2012).

Speaking on behalf of the Johannesburg Development Agency (JDA), Susan Monyai explained the dilemma: 'Sometimes we have projects that require specialised skills and we cannot therefore always employ local people'. (Interview: January 2012). A marketing manager at the JDA, Monyai pointed out that this insider-outsider conflict can also happen between different wards within Diepsloot: 'At other times,' she explained, 'people in ward X do not have the skills required and someone from ward Y is able to do the job, and then ward X people complain.' (ibid.)

Locals in Hermanus are similarly locked in a fierce competition for jobs. The 'outsiders' in this case are new arrivals, most of whom are apparently Xhosa speakers from the Eastern Cape. In a predominantly Coloured and Afrikaans-speaking community they stand out, and are differentiated even further by their separate residence in informal settlements. 'Insiders', or older residents, complain that the new arrivals are preferred over them for agricultural work. Locals do admit though that some of them shun the jobs because the farmers 'pay under the belt' (Focus group interviews: 13–14 December 2012).

In a community fraught with tense competition for employment, nepotism is commonly cited as a factor for some being employed and others being unemployed. Those in employment are said to recruit their own, either family members or 'home-boys'. It is worth noting that nepotism is alleged both within 'insiders' on the one hand, and between 'insiders' and 'outsiders' on the other hand. Insiders accuse others of giving preference to family members. 'Your child doesn't get a job,' explained one old resident, 'if your mother works there then she'll bring her sister's child in. But, your child can't get a job there.' (Focus group interviews: 13–14 December 2012).

New residents in Hermanus (Africans) accuse those in employment of recruiting employees from their own hometown. One explained how they are excluded from jobs as follows:

...as new residents, we stand no chance because if there are jobs

available, the ones that are already working are going to call on their relatives or the ones that they know for those opportunities. It is very difficult for most of the people that have just moved here. If you do not have a family around here or a family that has a family member that is working in that particular area, you are not going to get a job. The only chance that you will get is when the Whites come by and collect people to go, and for at least three weeks or so (Focus group interviews: 13–14 December 2012).

To stress the point, another new resident added that most African employees at the local municipality come from Engcobo. It is puzzling, he went on to explain, why the municipality even bothers to advertise the jobs. 'Forms are there for anyone to take and fill, but I can assure you, the person that you will see working there is either related or a friend to the people that are working there, it is not about knowing how to do the job but about who you know or how well connected you are' (ibid.). And home-boy ties also find expression in residential patterns. Home-boys are concentrated in certain parts of the community.

To be sure, views vary on nepotism. Some informants seem understanding and have resigned themselves to the practice. One Diepsloot resident pointed out:

Me, I see that the problem we are not finding jobs is because of nepotism. If you get a person you don't know, you will not get the job. You will get the job because the person in charge knows you. If they don't know you, things will not work out (Focus group interviews: 24–25 November 2012).

But, it should be done differently, another suggested:

People should be fair even though they have family members who also need jobs, whom they wind up doing favours for…they should take half of the people in need and then take half of their family members. Mix us, you see.

To others, nepotism remains objectionable. One likened it to apartheid:

They say Whites have apartheid…we have our own apartheid. How will we be equal if we still underestimate each other, if we still say I am Zulu, even when a job arises you want a Zulu person and you don't see the other person struggling next to you (Focus group interviews: 24–25 November 2012).

Whereas nepotism is blamed within groups, racism is alleged between groups. In Hermanus, Coloureds and Africans trade blame for their being unemployed. One employer is said to prefer one group, and the other another group. A local lady explained: 'Our men are sitting here. There are services outside: road maintenance; field maintenance; roads should be cleaned. Why can't the men get the jobs? Why not? Why can't my children get a job sweeping the streets? Why only Blacks?' (Focus group interviews: 13–14 December 2012).

Another old local resident added: 'I went to the municipality to look for work. I got there and filled in forms and waited, but because black people have the most options today, that fell away. They have the most options … They get first option … very unfair'. The incident seemed to resonate with others: 'It's true, because I also went to hand in my CV there. And when you go back, they've employed black people. These people aren't even from Hermanus. They come from the Eastern Cape and from Transkei' (ibid.).

Africans, too, have experienced similar instances of exclusion, for which they also allege racism. They can see signs of development in Hermanus, but they are not among the beneficiaries. Coloureds and Whites are benefiting instead, as one put it:

… there is that buzz of things happening, I can see things moving, but I do not see our kids being the ones that are working there. They are still sitting at home with their matric certificates, with their qualifications. I cannot see black people working but there is something happening. I can see most of the Whites working in town, I can see other races, but the black race, I am just wondering what is happening with us (ibid.).

The experience resonated with others:

I second what my sister just said, I cannot see development from the black side, and I can see other races moving and things happening on their side and nothing from our side. I can see the Foschinis and Edgars and people working there are Coloureds. We had our CV placed there, but they were not looked at. Even now when the Woolworths opened, we were there and were not even looked at. The only people that are looked at are Coloureds. Our CVs were sent there and we never received any communication from them, but we see the Coloureds are working now (ibid.).

Tension over employment has spilt over into social services. Housing is especially in demand. The demand not only stems from inward migration, but also from lay-offs in the agricultural sector. Once retrenched, workers vacate their farm residence and seek accommodation among locals in the community. This adds to the demand not only for employment, but also for housing. 'Way back,' one resident put it, 'there were only a few people who lived in Hermanus; there were enough houses for everyone. However, people moved here and they got houses. I don't want to mention names (ibid.).'

A popular feeling is that the newly arrived Africans are preferred over established, Coloured residents. One resident narrated her experience:

When I went and asked whether I could put my name on the list to get a house, I was told: 'Wait, just wait a bit'... Many of these people that come from outside, they have houses where they are from. They come here and overpopulate the area. As a result, the people from here become overcrowded in their homes. The children have children with these people, there are quite a few of these people (Focus group interviews: 13–14 December 2012).

Being overlooked for housing, it appears, at least according to the established residents, is symptomatic of a broader pattern. They charge that the general provision of social services mimics a similar pattern of discrimination. 'Zwelihle gets things that Mount Pleasant has been waiting on for 20 years and hasn't received,' said one resident in Hermanus and added: 'Genuine!' (ibid.). The sentiment proved popular and elicited a number of comments. 'Look,' started one resident, 'I'm going to be honest with you. Zwelihle receives bags and bags of food for their community (ibid.).' Another resident added, purporting to have witnessed it herself: 'It's true. I was down there last week. A huge truck came to deliver toys. I wish you could have seen the toys that those children received. What about our kids? They're not important to anybody' (ibid.).

Food and toys seem to be the tip of the iceberg. 'There are,' according to one resident:

> ...projects in Zwelihle but never here...they have that stuff for the children, 'Our School' or something...Yes, for the children. There are many such programmes. They keep the children out of trouble. On our side, there are no projects for children whose parents work; we do not know what the kids keep themselves busy with (Focus group interviews: 13–14 December 2012).

Another added: 'Look at their taxi-rank'. 'Exactly!' responded another and asked, 'Where's our taxi rank?' The answer to the question stressed their sense of injustice: 'They've got a smart taxi rank. Beautiful! They've got stalls. They have everything there. The facilities are lovely there. What do we have? Our people get soaking wet in the rain,' confirmed another resident (ibid.).

Though said to be favourites, Africans feel victimised and unwelcome in Hermanus. Their grievance, especially that of the new residents, is not only targeted at the Coloureds, but also at the established residents in general, including their fellow Africans. They accuse them of colluding with the authorities to cheat them out of housing. One resident explained that:

> ...if you are from the Eastern Cape, you do not have a house here, you can apply and the process gets done and when the houses are given out, your house will be given to a person that lives in the township here. You would see in the paper that a house is allocated to you; you will get a letter that says you have a house but you will not get that house (ibid.).

The resident then narrated a first-hand account:

> I know of a person that was in that situation, she went to the Housing Board in Cape Town and it was written that she had a house. She was told of her house and where it was. She went to that house but it was occupied by another person. She went back and was accompanied by a white person from the Housing Board who asked the occupant of the house how he came to be in the house because it was the other person's house (ibid.).

Aggravating their sense of mistreatment is an acute feeling of not belonging. They do not feel part of the community. An example of this exclusion, they cite, is the absence of a Xhosa radio channel. Not only does this make them feel unrecognised, but also starves them of information that may improve their lot. Explained one resident:

> It is from radio stations that we get to know of what other things the government is busy with and doing for the people. The programmes do get to the local government, but we are not exposed to them; we are not informed of them, and to worsen the situation, is that we are not able to get any information from the station because from the radio stations we get to know more about what the government is doing or wants to do for us and how we can participate in some of its programmes. I was in Cape Town when I heard on radio about some of the programmes for unemployed people, that there was something that they were going to get and they said that programme was going to start in George (Focus group interviews: 13–14 December 2012).

One resident further emphasised the disadvantage of being without a radio channel in their own language: 'From the radio, you get the numbers to call if you have questions, or if you want to have something clarified for you, but because we do not have that here, we are always not in the know' (ibid.). Instead of Umhlobo Wenene, the isiXhosa public station whose signal does not cover the area, they listen to Radio 2000, which they do not even understand because they 'are not educated. This is really hurting us, not being able to hear your own station is really a killer' (ibid.).

Diepsloot residents registered a similar concern, and pleaded for local radio stations: 'Even though I can't read, I have a vision that can contribute in developing the community as a whole. We mustn't think only one-sided. Educated people can read newspapers and all that, but how are you going to inform the person who is not educated?' (Focus group interviews: 24–25 November 2012.) Beyond it being a cultural affront, lack of a vernacular radio channel denies new residents useful information that can improve their plight. Because they are indigent, they rely and look up to the State to provide social relief and opportunities. And radio is useful to communicate such messages.

So, the competition for services and jobs is a cause of racial tension. This is exacerbated by a sense of discrimination. Africans feel they are treated as the unequal 'other'. One African man, Ofentse, for instance, spoke about how his daughter arrived home one day with a notice (letter) inviting parents to a school governing meeting. The note, however, was written in Afrikaans, which incensed him. He immediately went to the school to confront the principal and demanded that a note addressed to him be written in isiXhosa: 'I had enough of sitting through meetings with this principal conducting parent-teacher meetings in Afrikaans and not even English and without a Xhosa translator – as if we do not exist'. After the confrontation the principal subsequently issued all public notices to parents in all three languages but the situation remains somewhat tense (Fieldwork notes: 22 March 22 – 13 April 2012).

And the resentment extends towards Whites, too. In this case, it is stoked by inequality. Coloureds and Africans are scrambling over the same scarce services, whilst Whites live a relatively comfortable lifestyle. One resident put it thus:

> *To give you an example of this apartheid that I am talking about, I have been here for a long time and when it comes to housing, it is a very big issue because getting a house here is not just possible. I can understand that one can be without a job, but one has to have something, at least, let there be a land where one can have a house or can live from. The government has sold our land. Looking at the areas where Boers live, they have plenty space to themselves and we are living in shacks. I mean, us that are in majority are the ones that are living in shacks and living in those shacks comes at a price because one, there is no electricity. In the white areas they have all these things that make their lives much better, and even if they are faced with problems they still find comfort in that they have a place to put their heads on, they have space for a growing family and that is the direct opposite to our case. Yes, this is what I have noted and I realise that it is a growing trend* (Focus group interviews: 13–14 December 2012).

Contrasted against the general state of life among Africans and Coloureds, the sense of inequality is glaring. According another resident:

> *…the areas that we are living in are not clean; it is dirty. The water we have used in the house is thrown out next to the shacks we are living in and the toilets we are using are communal, anyone and everyone can use them at any time and to some extent, anyhow. The saddest part is that we are not working. And when we connect electricity, they come and they*

cut it because we are bridging and that means we do not have electricity Focus group interviews: 13–14 December 2012).

Even more disconcerting for Coloured residents of Hawston (in Hermanus) is that the prosperity of Whites threatens their own shelter and well-being. Their community is surrounded by wealthy property owners. And more continue to arrive. Consequently, prices for land have gone up, beyond the purchasing power of the locals. They cannot buy land beyond their communities and have to make do with the land they already have. Because families continue to expand, this poses a serious danger for the future. One local leader put it thus:

The plots are so expensive. That means that the man from Joburg or from Pretoria or The Netherlands can afford it. Not us. Make it possible. Have a decent price so that we can also buy them. I have five children to raise; I can't live in one little house for five children. Sell the plots at a price that we, too, can afford. But we're being pushed back. We must go to Kawyderskraal. My son is 23. Say he gets married in seven years. There won't be anymore land left because they're building golf courses. Golf courses won't benefit us. The whole of Hawston can fit onto the area that they want to build a golf course on (Focus group interviews: 13–14 December 2012).

No less exasperating for one local leader is what he considers the duplicitous manner in which they are coaxed to sell their land. The municipality, he explains, contends that the land they seek is not suitable for human habitation. Instead of the residential place, they will set up recreational activities, namely golf. But, the local leader is not convinced:

They say it's 'wasteland'. But the mayor's house is built on that 'wasteland' in Vermont. Can you tell me that those wealthy people won't build houses of R3 million or R4 million on that golf course? Will it still be 'wasteland' then? Then after the golf course it's R3.5 million for a rugby field (ibid.).

If not by underplaying the value of the land, the local leader went on to explain, the municipality asked them to trade their land in return for recreational facilities. The offer of a trade-off was similarly unconvincing. He insisted that recreational facilities are a standard municipal service to residents. They did not have to give up a precious commodity such as land for what should be their right as citizens:

> *Why must they give us money for sports grounds only if we hand over the land for a golf course? Hermanus and Mount Pleasant and other areas have sports grounds which are maintained. Now if we don't want the golf course they withdraw the funding. This golf course issue – they didn't acknowledge the community. And you have to consult the community. So last year the municipality just wanted to shove the golf course down our throats and we just have to accept that. Now we speak our minds and we're 'hooligans' and 'barbarians'. I want to be honest. You must say it the way it is* (Focus group interviews: 13–14 December 2012).

Rather than fanciful arguments, developers and property seekers have simply offered handsome payments for the houses. 'Say you're struggling,' one resident began her own story, 'there's no work, nothing. And a white man comes and offers you a lot of money for your property. What choice do you have?' It turned out she was offered money to sell her property. 'That happened to me. R950 000 – I almost peed in my pants. And all I saw was that money. I thought I would just take the money and buy myself a little RDP house. Then I thought, no man! (ibid.).'

Though in need of money, the locals, like wealthy property seekers, treasure the scenic sight and the pleasure of their natural surroundings. The residents that were offered money refused to sell 'because when we wake up we will find that we can't access our own beaches anymore … yes. These rich people will build a high wall around the place. Then our people have to pay R25 or R35 to have access to our own beach'. Actually, local residents, because of their scenic views, think developers are in cahoots with the municipality to drive them off their land, a situation they are determined to resist. One even warned of a menacing future: 'They want to steal our land to the white man. They are depriving our people because they want to drive us off our land. Terrible things are going to happen here ... because they are fighting us over our land' (Focus group interviews: 13–14 December 2012).

According to one fisherman, this is 'the municipality's strategy to force [them] to go to Kawyderskraal … a place on the other side of the mountain'. Property seekers are thus seen in dim light. Locals do not consider selling their own properties a normal financial transaction. The offers to purchase, according to them, are predicated on malice. This has to do with commercial developments around the area that have left a sour taste in their mouths. A resident narrated one incident:

> *Look at what they're doing to us. I have been camping from six months old. My parents took us camping. You were propped up with pillows and a foam mattress. I am now 43 years old. Suddenly, for the past two or three years we are no longer allowed to camp at the* vlei. *Now you can see what these people are up to. When Arabella was built, suddenly we weren't good enough. Because it was built for the very rich and they don't want their guests to have a view of our old, windswept tents. White people's dogs are more important than what we, as human beings, are. Those people walk their dogs there early in the morning and they take pictures of our tents and stuff and put it in The Times and complain about us. Where were these white people when we were camping there all the years?* (13–14 December 2012).

Commercial developments have had an uneven impact, with racial undertones. White investors have flourished while the locals are denied a livelihood. Locals used to fish at the *vlei* (mentioned above), but the construction of the plush Arabella Country Club changed that. Access was blocked, with devastating consequences:

> *Have you ever heard of a white person drowning in the* vlei? *You've never heard of that. My uncle's nephews ... Coloured ... have drowned in that* vlei. *Because they were catching fish. They had nets there. When Whites came there they removed their nets. Now people had to go out at night to catch fish. Now they had to steal fish at night with their nets. And the little boat capsized and they drowned, which was very unnecessary. We have to die in order to put some food on the table. They think nothing of us. There was a woman...Ingrid what's-her-name...she spent hundreds of rands closing up the entrance to the* vlei *so that we can't get access. It's all about Arabella!* (ibid.).

In other words, the popular feeling is that white developers are exploiting local, natural resources for their own enrichment. And they deliberately prohibit locals benefiting from similar resources, even though they are natural endowments, to which no one can lay prior ownership. To emphasise the point about uneven development, another resident made an example about the white sea-sand and grit. 'I was six years old when my mother died,' she began the story and continued:

> we used to fetch bags and bags of grot[1] at the back there to put on her grave, to prevent weeds and flowers growing through it. Now you need a permit for that, too. As soon as the white man sees we are busy with this and that...If they see people are busy building and they are collecting white sand, then law enforcement makes them unload that sand again. I have white sea sand in my garden. I need a permit for that, too. And I found it there! (Focus group interviews: 13–14 December 2012).

Even *konfyt*, another resident added, has been commercialised for the benefit of a few:

> I have [konfyt] growing in my yard but I need a permit to pick it. As soon as a white man sees he can make money out of something, then you need a permit for it. They must just still get a permit for Coloured people. If they see they can make 'bokvet' out of Coloured people then they will impose a permit on Coloured people (ibid.).

Needless to say, locals have become hostile against commercial developers. 'They must stop taking advantage of our ignorance. Because our people are ignorant and didn't go to school they think they can walk all over us,' quips one resident. Though reluctant to sell, they still reckon that what they are offered is a lot less than the value of the land. They seemed to have learnt from previous developments, which promised much but offered very little, as one of them explained:

> Now a hotel like Arabella comes along. We stay with a mop and a broom in our hands. We don't just want to clean and make up beds. We also want to be directors and that. Take us up with you. Make us directors and what's-the-name too ... shareholders. Really! Mop and sweep and make up beds. Oh no, take us up with you (ibid.).

Conversely, Petsana and Mhlontlo did not suffer any such social fissures. Their relative obscurity and economic marginality do not make them

---

1. Small, gravel-like stones

attractive to foreign nationals or rich developers. The few foreign nationals that have gone to Mhlontlo, for instance, do not seem to be competing with the locals for jobs, but are self-employed as traders. The presence of foreign traders has played out quite differently in Mhlontlo, and Diepsloot in particular, as we discuss below.

What the foregoing also underscores is the intense reliance on the State for a livelihood. The desperation is that it even incites tension among residents, and between local-born and foreign-born residents. Consequently, residents are beginning to 'take care of their own'. Nepotism, which in this case not only implies kin relations, but also friends and political supporters, becomes a way of life to survive. This then creates a permissible climate for patronage-politics. It includes the formation of lobby groups to secure scarce resources and services normally provided by the State. Such lobby groups do not provide service for altruistic reasons. Rather, they are themselves a source of living for their leaders. They use them to secure patronage.

Also noteworthy here is the seeming bias of the Overstrand Municipality towards its affluent citizens. It seems more keen in advancing interests of property developers and the established fishing industry than those of local fishermen, who seem confined to the subsistence level. What seems to be municipal support for property and commercial development raises questions over its embeddedness within commercial interests, especially because it seems willing to relegate its poor residents to the margins of socio-economic life. Could the municipal zeal to promote commercial interest derive from something other than ensuring development for the community?

SURVIVAL STRATEGIES

Overall, the study reveals that whereas some have sought employment from the State, others have resorted to self-employment. Locals have devised various economic and income-generating initiatives. These initiatives have had contradictory results. They alienated some locals further away from foreign nationals, while other locals have made common cause with foreign nationals because of a shared economic interest. The response of officialdom has also brought into question the effectiveness of their policy regime in both aiding and facilitating self-generated local economic activity.

Informal Trading

Spaza shops and street vending stalls are a common economic activity for self-sustenance. They are especially ubiquitous in Diepsloot. They sell foodstuffs and other basic necessities such as cigarettes, mobile phone services, etc. While *spaza* shops may be considered a source of living, street vending is simply a survival strategy.

As a subsistence activity, vendors do not make a profit, but make enough to live off. For Diepsloot vendors there are also many obstacles. Diepsloot does not seem to have wholesalers where they can stock up. 'You can only find shops in Alexandra,' remarked one vendor. 'So if there are people who want to invest here, it would be better even for us with small business, we might be able to get the stock there. It would make our lives easier.' Not only do they expend more on transportation to get stock, their market is also fluid. Public gatherings, such as sports activities on a makeshift field, provided a lucrative market. Such activities have become fewer:

> For instance, if there is a match I can be able to sell peanuts, for example, that is also a creative way of doing business. We used to have such facilities but they were stopped because they are building schools and houses, so that we could also be developed as a community. ...all-round sport, we used to play soccer, netball, basketball and indoor games. But education takes priority over other things (Focus group interviews: 24–25 November 2012).

Local government has sought to provide some assistance. The shelters provided by the municipality, for example, have been quite useful. 'Now it is better,' says one vendor, and explains further, 'because before we used to knock off early, especially when it is hot or raining, but now we can continue selling our food until half past nine and go back to our houses with the money we made from the sales.' Others have found regulations in some instances quite restraining, however. Municipalities require vendors to obtain permits and can only sell in designated spots. Failure to secure one, or trading outside the designated area, meets with severe punishment. Their goods are confiscated. One vendor explained their plight:

> ...we want to be self-employed, but the by-laws are also enforced. Like he said, there is a lot of competition in selling, but there is only minimal space allocated to certain people for selling, about 10 or 11 people. Where

*are the rest of us supposed to go? Because there is no other place to go
to…*

*How would I know that I'm standing on the wrong place, because I
am only trying to make a living? You see that is contradicting because
when I try to make a living they take my goods away. So what is the
solution – resorting to crime? And, when I am doing crime it will take
them a long time to find me because they will have to investigate first*
(Focus group interviews: 24–25 November 2012).

Even those with permits complain that the municipality operates in an
inconsiderate manner. Municipalities do not inform vendors beforehand
about operations that might disrupt their business. For instance, '…when we
are busy selling on the street,' said one vendor, 'they sometimes remove us
when they want to install pipes'. He explained further:

*…we only see things happening, e.g. sometimes the Red Ants will come
here to dig, they won't even tell us how long that is going to take. And
that is bad for business because we don't even know whether they are
going to take a week/month/year, they also don't give us options to, or
maybe give us a temporary space where we can continue to run our
businesses* (Focus group interviews: 24–25 November 2012).

If not by inconsiderate behaviour, vendors are inconvenienced by erratic
municipal services. Water cut-offs or electricity outages bring business to a
halt. One vendor explained the inconvenience: 'We have a bakery here, and
there is always power failure. They don't inform us when there will be no
electricity; it comes and goes as it pleases. Especially when there is wind and
when it's raining then we are unable to continue doing our work'.

Though appreciative of the assistance provided by the municipality,
vendors plead that they should get both alerts beforehand, and
uninterrupted services. A major suggestion, though, is that the State provides
them with both financial assistance and facilities to do business. 'If I have
enough money, I can expand my business by buying more stock. That will be
the way to expand the business,' noted one and expanded:

*I think it's better if the money comes from the government for shelter. Say
the government can subsidise with half of the money. Because at the
moment we are using other people's money and the money keeps on*

increasing. And there are many challenges involving the money; there are many things that could happen, but at the end of the day the person wants the money as it is (Focus group interviews: 24–25 November 2012).

Another added:

Say maybe I have certain skills. Like sewing. I could find a place where I can hire people to work with so that we could be able to reduce the rate of crime, because at the moment there are a lot of people who are unemployed and the rate of crime is very high because of that. We don't have powers to find a work place for ourselves to do that; the problem is money to buy material and the machinery to start business. Maybe if government can come, in that matter by giving us the opportunities to sew clothes for certain departments, that could enable me to find/hire people to work for me, by so doing crime can be reduced (ibid.).

Foreign nationals are also giving local vendors serious competition. At the beginning, one vendor pointed out, South Africans dominated the informal trade business in Diepsloot: 'This has changed now and the foreigners are the ones who dominate informal trade' (Fieldwork notes: January 2012). A Zimbabwean woman named Diasy is one of the many such hawkers. Diasy has a stall set up outside Johannesburg Water, a water purification plant on the outskirts of Diepsloot. She sells cigarettes, sweets, peanuts and fruit. It is an isolated place, far from the settlement where a lot of people are about, but she is the only hawker servicing a workforce of about 100 people working at the plant, who live in a hostel nearby. Very uncomfortable, she kept looking over her shoulder, probably worried a police vehicle or some state officials would appear to arrest her (for not having proper papers, perhaps).

Diasy came to South Africa in 2005, fleeing political troubles in her native Zimbabwe. She moved in with her sister who was already in South Africa, in Skotiphola. She left Skotiphola when people there were removed to make way for the development of Cosmo City in 2008. She now lives in a backyard shack in Diepsloot. She claims she does not have much of a social life, but goes to church on Sundays. Diasy's family, including her daughter, live in Zimbabwe and her only relative in Diepsloot is her sister. She feels South Africans treat foreigners with disdain, and she cannot wait to get back home permanently as soon the political situation stabilises there.

Another foreign born vendor is Donald, a young Mozambican. He sells oranges on a busy street corner, adjacent to a taxi car wash. Donald has been living in Diepsloot for 14 months. His mother died when he was a toddler and he was raised by his maternal grandmother. His half-brother owns a *spaza* shop in Diepsloot, and sent for him to come and work here. He sells oranges at a very cheap price (at 50c an orange or a 15-orange packet for R5). Donald has a couple of hangers-on, including South Africans from Bolobedi in Limpopo. They offer him protection from would-be bullies or those who would take advantage of his vulnerable status, and in return they help themselves to the oranges and sometimes get some oranges on credit for their girlfriends. Donald's day starts at 7 AM when he packs the oranges onto the back of a van to set up his stall at 'his' corner by 8 AM. He works until he has sold out, which on a slow day means going home at 8 or even 9 AM.

Informal trading in Diepsloot did not seem to be a major source of tension among locals and foreign nationals. The fortunes of one do not seem to be affected by the presence of the other. The dynamic is different higher up, among owners of *spaza* shops. The presence of immigrant owned *spaza* shops is not itself the cause of tension. Rather, local traders complain of being crowded out by immigrant owned businesses. Dennis Mathebula, a local businessman and chairman of the Diepsloot ANC branch, pointed out that at least 14 shops on his street, JB Marks, are said to be owned by Somali businessmen: 'I am showing you this thing, my brother,' Dennis complained as he gestured down the street, 'so that you can see for yourself. The Somalis have taken over Diepsloot' (Fieldwork notes: July 2012).

Local traders say they simply cannot compete with their foreign born counterparts. They band together and buy in bulk, a practice that earns them huge discounts, which enables them to sell their products cheaper than their local counterparts. The locals, even though they hold negative perceptions about foreigners, and lament how South African *spazas* and other informal business owners are driven out of business by the foreigners, confess without hesitation that they patronise Pakistani and Somali businesses because of their cheap prices. One local added: 'Also, they close late.' Locally owned *spazas*, even if one wanted to support local businesses, close early. Because they open until late, Pakistani, Somali or Ethiopian traders offer a convenient service.

In an area that lacks jobs, employment patterns in foreign owned *spazas* sharpen the local grievance against immigrant traders. The accusation is that they prefer to employ 'their own' over locals, and thus do not promote local development. Dennis explains: 'All the established guys live in Johannesburg, Fordsburg, or Pretoria. They don't invest here. Their money does not circulate within Diepsloot'. When they employ staff other than their Muslim or Ethiopian nationals, these entrepreneurs prefer employing young foreign girls from Zimbabwe or Mozambique. 'They are working for their people. Our people are not benefiting,' laments the businessman (Fieldwork notes: July 2012).

Of the 15 *spaza* shops or grocery shop owners/employees interviewed, only one employed a black South African, a young woman with a baby on her back. The rest of the businesses interviewed employed foreign nationals, from the same country as the owner. Mr Dalmar, a Somali immigrant who arrived in Diepsloot in 2007, and is employed by a fellow countryman, proffers an explanation. Muslims, he intimates, have an obligation towards other Muslims and it is good for business: 'They do not steal,' Mr Dalmar says. He ascribes this to the harsh punishment meted out to thieves in his culture, and how that curtails crime.

Another explanation for employing locals, especially women, is offered by Mr Dalmar. The gentleman, a Pakistani national who arrived in South Africa in 2009, manages a grocery shop owned by a fellow countryman. The shop also sells electronic wares and fixes mobile phone devices. Though it is one of the few shops that employs a local, an African woman, Dalmar's views of women, however, reveal a general prejudice against employing women. He believes that women should stay at home. 'Women are not allowed in the street. They go to the street only if they are going to work or to school.' He talks about the 'loose way' women in Diepsloot (or South Africa) carry themselves. In his culture, he points out, women must cover themselves. 'Here in South Africa women walk around naked,' Mr Dalmar spits out as he explains passionately (Fieldwork notes: June 2012).

According to Dennis Mathebula, concerns about the proliferation of foreign owned businesses were raised as early as 2004. A memorandum of understanding (MoU) was drawn up and signed, according to which foreign owned shops would not exceed 19 shops in Diepsloot. This agreement was to be effective only in ward 95, then under Councillor Madlozi Mahlangu's tenure. The MoU was never implemented. Nor are pleas made to the Somali Forum of Traders, to limit their presence and employ locals, likely to be heeded. In an attempt to help out the local traders, the North West Township (NORWETO) Chamber of Commerce invited a representative of the Somali Forum of Traders to one meeting to convey their complaints. But the foreign representative reported that he was battling to dissuade his members from operating multiple shops within a concentrated space. According to the representative, they insist that South Africa is a free enterprise country, which permits them to set up as many shops as they want.

Overlooking locals for employment has only accentuated an existing cultural schism between locals and immigrants. While a few of the foreign nationals interviewed have acquired proficiency in one of the local languages, a predominant sentiment is that most immigrants keep to themselves. Conversely, what locals consider aloofness, according to Mr Dalmar, foreign nationals see as South Africa's tolerance of cultural and religious diversity, an endearing quality about this country. Before coming to South Africa, en route from Pakistan, Dalmar had settled in Europe and then North Africa. He hated the assimilationist attitudes of the French in France and of North Africans when he stopped over there. He finds South Africans more accommodating of diversity. 'In Europe your life is difficult. Children cannot go to school. You can't drive, "Where is your licence?" They hate your children. You must pray at home,' he shares this litany of cultural and religious intolerance in Europe. 'Here in Diepsloot, it is good.'(Fieldwork notes: June 2012.)

What foreigners regard as an expression of their own culture, some locals dismiss angrily as 'arrogance' towards South Africans. 'They are happy to get our money but they do not mix with us, they think they are better than us,' said a South African customer who came to buy milk from a grocery shop during one interview. This has obviously made local traders objects of local resentment and possible targets of attack. They live under a constant threat of attack, to which they've responded by looking at ways to secure protection – something that is looked at further, below.

As noted earlier in the case of customers, not all locals are inconvenienced by foreign born traders. Some local property owners have also taken advantage of the presence of immigrant traders as an opportunity to break into the real estate business. They rent out their premises to immigrants even elbowing out the local business owners in Diepsloot. Even ordinary homeowners have taken advantage of the opportunity. They start off by renting out space in their houses to Somali shop owners, and eventually move out of the houses and collect rents from these businesses, while renting a shack in someone else's yard or move back 'home' (the place they had migrated from), collecting passive income.

Two informants, one a direct beneficiary of this arrangement, explained how the arrangement works. Homeowners grant occupation rights to houses (sometimes shacks) to these traders (at prices ranging from R10 000 to R15 000) in private transactions involving no legal precepts. In addition, property owners pocket about R2,000 per month in rental from the business. Meanwhile, the original owners continue to hold the legal ownership rights to their properties.

Sometimes, once the trader has thus 'acquired' the structure, they will promptly build additional rooms (sometimes upstairs above the original structure), which they use as their living quarters. One interviewee explained further:

> Then they save more money because they don't have to travel any distance from the shop. That is why they are the last shops to close at night; and when you need something early in the morning they are already open. Sometimes, if you are desperate, some will open after they have closed to sell you something. So the people prefer these ones (Interview: January 2012).

The 'rent-seeking' practice is so rife that the Chamber even resolved to meet with the housing MEC to determine the extent of the problem and work out a strategy to confront it. Evidently, not all locals are affected similarly by the presence of foreign traders. Some benefit, whilst others lose out. Hostility towards foreigners was palpable, nonetheless.

Unlike Diepsloot, Overstrand, Petsana/Maluti or Mhlontlo do not have similar tensions among local traders. This does not, however, suggest an absence of foreign owned *spazas*. Mhlontlo, for instance, does have a few in the area; they include one from Somalia, another from Pakistan, and a couple from Zimbabwe.

Maxamed Shermarke, for instance, is from Mogadishu, in the Kismanyo district of the war ravaged Somalia. Maxamed claims to be a teacher by profession, but, due to the absence of government in Somalia, he has no papers to prove it. South Africa's openness attracted him to the country. South Africa, alongside Libya and Saudi Arabia, are popular (immigrant) destinations in Mogadishu. For him, however, discrimination put him off Saudi Arabia, whilst Libya's undemocratic regime made the country unappealing.

South Africa was most attractive, and he got here in 1994, on election day, just as the country was becoming a democracy. He still remembers fondly, watching long queues of voters on television. From Johannesburg, he took a bus to Port Elizabeth where he worked for an 'Indian' shop owner. Among the customers there were people from the former Transkei, who regaled him about the beauty of their countryside. That got him to relocate to Qumbu – its rural life reminded him of home. He insists, though, that he is tired of the life of a refugee and wants to go back home.

Another is Maghdud Khel from Chak Basawa, in the Mandibhadin district of Pakistan. He was fresh from high school when he took the decision to come to South Africa. He wanted to lead an independent life and a friend of his was already in South Africa. He came to the country in 2010, flying to Mozambique via Dubai and Kenya. He came to Qumbu because his friend had already established a shop there, selling and repairing mobile phones. A few months later he opened up his own *spaza* shop, after taking an offer from a Mr Makinana, a former shopkeeper and a client at the mobile phone shop, to become a tenant.

Maghdud enjoys cordial relations with locals. This is partly because of his relations with them. He gives customers grocery items on credit, and they pay him on 'pay day'. An indication of the good relations, according to Maghdud, is that locals, especially his neighbours, look out for him. In one instance, neighbours foiled a break-in into his shop. As burglars attempted to break into the shop whilst Maghdud was inside, he rang Mr Makinana, who then alerted the neighbours. One of the neighbours fired a gunshot into the air, and the burglars fled. Maghdud has no intention to go back to Pakistan.

Mhlontlo also hosts a couple from Zimbabwe, Martin and Mervis Dube. They came into South Africa by foot, walking through the southern parts of Mozambique. After walking through KwaZulu-Natal for 38 days, they settled in Qumbu. Martin does upholstery for a living while Mervis is a housewife looking after their children. He works on the client's premises. They are always on the move because they follow business all the time. When they do not get further business in Qumbu, they will move again.

Lack of hostility towards immigrant traders in Mhlontlo suggests that they do not pose a threat to local traders. In any case, there seemed to be a marginal presence of local traders, which makes immigrant traders quite valuable to local consumers. It is quite curious, though, that an area including Petsana, with such high rates of unemployment, as noted above, would show such dim signs of self-initiatied income generation. The question is, were there no local efforts towards such? Or could it be that where they were initiated, they simply failed? These questions are explored further below.

In the case of Diepsloot, however, locals faced with unemployment have taken it upon themselves to find ways of making a living. The strategies vary. Some have opted to engage in trade, while others have resorted to renting out their own properties to traders. Lack of regulations, however, has seen local traders facing stiff challenges from immigrant traders. Appeals to the State for some form of regulation do not seem to have yielded any meaningful responses. Local traders are quite convinced, though, that without any State regulation (or support) their businesses face a dim future.

PROMOTING LOCAL ECONOMIC AND INCOME-GENERATING ACTIVITIES

Scrutiny of official measures to promote local economic activity reveals a mixed picture characterised by unequal treatment, possible corruption, and sheer neglect. And the extent to which official measures have any impact is largely determined by the economic opportunities presented by each locality.

Where a locality is endowed with natural resources, such as Overstrand's access to fishing and Mhlontlo's communal/agricultural land, official measures stand a chance of registering some success. Ideally, both the land and the ocean are a sustainable source of livelihood. Fishing and farming are potential economic activities. Availability, however, does not presuppose access, nor does it necessarily imply natural resources are utilised optimally. Whether or not locals exploit natural resources to eke out a meaningful livelihood depends not only on individual/community initiative, but also on an enabling resource base and a legislative framework.

Fishing is restricted. Some areas are closed off completely to fishing, and others require a permit. This is apparently meant to avoid fish becoming extinct due to overfishing. Local fishermen do not agree with the restrictions; reasons for their disagreement vary. First, they regard the ocean as a natural endowment. 'The sea belongs to no one,' one of them maintains. 'It belongs to God.' Fishermen have little sympathy for conservation schemes to replenish endangered species. Instead, they 'demand free – universal access!' Susan Swanepoel, Secretary of the Fishers Forum and Ward 9 community representative, and serving member of the Community Policing Forum (CPF), dismisses such schemes as 'an environmental, scientific-conservationist ploy to deprive fishers from food, subsistence, livelihoods, and commercial opportunities, which is also aimed at denying fishers access to the resource' (Fieldwork notes: 22 March – 13 April 2012).

Generations of families have historically lived off the ocean. One of them is Orbert van Wyk's family. Orbert's father had his own fishing boat and crew. When a demand for abalone started in Kleinmond in the 1960s, he bought three boats and had his own crew of divers. In 1984 he sold his boats and diving equipment. Years later, in 1998, Orbert's family decided to apply for fishing rights. But the application was declined and many others (individually and collectively) were declined. Orbert is enraged by what he feels is an injustice:

> *None of my brothers, sisters or children holds fishing rights currently–this really hurts because it was because of my grandfather's vision and skills transfer that many fishers entered this industry and they can all benefit today and into the future* (Fieldword notes: 22 March – 13 April 2012).

Failure to secure a licence is an obvious cause of bitterness, as it denies a source of livelihood. Orbert's bitterness, however, has more to do with a sense of unfairness in how licences are granted. He ascribes his unsuccessful applications to 'jealousy and in-fighting'. He says: 'Historical beneficiaries like us will not benefit from the proposed new legislation because gatekeepers make decisions on who will benefit from, and receive, fishing rights!' The State, according to Orbert is not blameless. Licensing is fraught with 'patronage, nepotism, corruption and maladministration, and the government is unable to contain or eradicate these policy fault lines' (ibid.).

Oletta and Olivia, both of whom were born in Hawston into 'a strong traditional fishing family (10 children) history', with 'fish and abalone as their staple food' (Fieldwork notes: 22 March – 13 April 2012), hold a similar sentiment as Obert. They charge that quotas are allocated on a 'buddy-buddy' system, or for specific individuals (gate-keepers) only – for example even gangsters in Hawston have fishing quotas – while their historical (traditional) subsistence rights have been revoked because they are black women.

They, too, want the fishing rights that were held by their parents (who have since died) restored to them. Indeed, allegations of corruption in the issuing of licences are prominent. This suggests that the issuing of licences is not governed strictly by regulation, but also by one's ability to pay bribes.

Oletta and Olivia went on to complain that because fishing has traditionally been a men's activity, they're especially denied licences because they're women. They have now resorted to forming a co-operative 'to pursue their collective and individual fishing rights (quota) as women!' Fisherwomen do seem a rarity indeed. One fisherwoman, who describes herself as 'the only white woman with fishing rights since 2003 till 2012', complains that boats are not convenient for women. She shares the same ablution amenities as men, an experience she finds unbearable: 'Currently there is no mercy for women on the sea'. She insists that the fishing industry must be open and sensitised to the needs of women: 'Women need to get more involved in fishing … therefore we need changes to the Act, we need better facilities, we need training, women must get more involved with the sea, because it is not the exclusive domain of men!' (Fieldwork notes: 22 March – 13 April 2012.)

Thus the criteria for granting a fishing licence are not only murky, but the industry itself is prejudicial against women. Where fish is the major source of livelihood, gender prejudice feminises poverty. This is symptomatic of what most locals feel is the bigger problem about the fishing industry, racial prejudice. Blacks are criminalised, while whites appear to be advantaged (as we discuss further below).

Without a licence to fish, says one fisherman, 'they're making criminals out of us'. The ocean, he continues, is full not only of 'abalone and crayfish', but also 'its white mussels, its catfish…you name it. It's all there. Divide it up. Give us all a piece to survive. Why must we steal'? The fisherman is emphatic that 'they don't have another choice. They have to steal'. He then explains how the loot is sold and the proceeds thereof:

> They sell it to the people from Cape Town that live here in town. I charge R200. Then there's a man from Worcester. He also buys. Then I have to give the boatman and the guy that carries it around R50 to R80. And the rest is mine. And that's just for tonight (Focus group interviews: 13–14 December 2012).

As a result of poaching activity, any Coloured or African man along the coast is considered a potential criminal. 'When a Boer sees you here at Sun Park, in no time,' says one fisherman, 'there will be police all over the place, particularly around you'. He elaborates:

> They will be asking what do you want here and they will be rude and eventually manhandle you. This happens to a black person and the Boers

will be loafing around and nothing will be done to them, they will never be asked silly questions and manhandled (Focus group interviews: 13–14 December 2012).

Another emphasises: 'And they just report us Coloureds. If you go to Vermont and you're wearing a wetsuit, they don't even know whether you're going to surf or not, they just call the cops'. White guys, however, the respondents believe, are treated differently, even though they may also be involved in poaching, as one explained:

These white people are the ones who steal legally. They also steal but they call us 'thieves'. But because our skin colour is different they call the cops. And the police act on whatever they tell them. I was in Vermont once and I could see how these white guys were poaching. And I was thinking to myself: If these were Coloureds they would have called the cops (ibid.).

The fishing industry, the fishermen contend, is skewed in favour of the established companies. Licensed fishermen, because they don't own a boat, for instance, make less money. One fisherman explains it as follows:

Our people go to sea and catch fish. If you earn R300 per day you're lucky. The boatman must subtract his petrol money; you have to pay the skipper and then you have to pay the bakkie-boy. So you're lucky if you earn between R250 and R300 a day. If you buy electricity of R100 you get so few units. Then you have to have food for tonight and bread money for tomorrow (ibid.).

Conversely, where natural resources to exploit are non-existent, such as in Petsana and Maluti, locals depend entirely on state generated economic activities. Here there is a much greater expectation on the State to provide opportunities. Locals have especially been encouraged to form co-operatives. Mme (Mrs) Paballo, of Paballo Co-operatives in Petsana, is one of the locals who responded to the call to form co-operatives. She has registered 19 co-operatives and serves as chairperson for the CPF in Nketoana. Those who formed co-operatives were informed that they will be awarded contracts to do work with the municipality. That promise, however, never materialised. 'When there is work that could easily be carried out by a co-operative', Mme Paballo explains, 'the municipality awards the work to a CK (company).

There was an event in which co-operatives were invited, but the municipality invited CK' (Interview: 8 December 2011).

Together with other women, Mme Paballo initiated a factory to manufacture toilet paper in 2005. But the municipality did not support her, neither was it interested in providing a site for the operation of the factory. She had to rent out a place at higher cost. Since 2006 to the present, there has been no work or contract from municipalities given to co-operatives, she explained:

> The problem is that the province and region are not exerting sufficient pressure on municipalities to prioritise co-operatives. The most feasible project that could be carried out by the co-operatives is the school feeding scheme. This project is not being handed to co-operatives because school principals have vested interest in companies that get tenders to provide the services (Interview: 8 December 2011).

A sense of betrayal has consequently emerged that officials encouraged people to form co-operatives, but contracts and tenders are not awarded to local co-operatives. In fact, a local economic development office was recently opened. The delay could have been caused by other factors, but it possibly suggests lacklustre interest in involving co-operatives in local economic activities. Rather, their approach to local economic development and poverty alleviation has largely taken the form of indigent programmes and providing discounts for residents who are unable to afford their rates. In turn, this encourages indebtedness towards local politicians, some of whom manipulate for their own ends.

PRESENCE AND STATE OF THE LOCAL STATE

Inadequate official measures to promote local economic development belie a state that is generally responsive and present in society. Social grants are widely spread out and relatively easily accessible to South Africa's poor. Social services, albeit unevenly provided or accessible, are generally present in the various communities from rural to urban communities, including in informal settlements.

Diepsloot, an informal settlement, is a telling example of the penetrative reach of the State into society. Informal settlements are often characterised as no man's land, neglected by the State with very minimal, or an absence of services. Because of high levels of poverty, unemployment and squalor, they are the usual flashpoints of violent 'service delivery protests', ghastly crimes and lawlessness.

But unlike the pre-Lula *favelas* of Brazil, or the apartheid-era 'squatter camps', where government response to the 'malaise' was forced removals or attempts at gentrification (as in military ruled Brazil in the 1970s), the ANC government has adopted a different approach towards informal settlements. It is cognisant of the adverse impact of apartheid spatial engineering and its impoverishing effect on the black majority, and has thus sought a way to fast track access to services in these areas, speed up the construction of low-cost housing and, most importantly, integrate these communities in the wider economic hubs on whose peripheries they exist. In the Gauteng Province, Diepsloot is among the chosen sites for such initiatives.

Government has experimented with different approaches to addressing, for instance, the housing backlog in Diepsloot. The so-called Peoples Housing Process (PHP), in terms of which government gave subsidies of R7,500 for every house built by an individual potential homeowner, was the first such attempt. Deemed too slow in yielding the desired results, the PHP was soon replaced in 1999 by the introduction of the subsidised 'RDP' houses. The RDP housing programme was supplemented with the provision of bonded houses, a more formalised development with in-house amenities such as electricity, running water, toilets, and tarred roads. According to the Affordable Land & Housing Data Centre (ALHDC), the number of formal residential properties in Diepsloot exceeded 6,915 by the end of 2011.

Despite these attempts, however, the ever increasing numbers of people moving into Diepsloot, coupled with bureaucratic lags, simply overwhelms the State's capacity to provide adequate housing. Challenges are also felt in the area of electricity and health. Most of the households in Diepsloot do not have electricity. Households with electricity are those found in the bonded housing section of Tanganani (extension 3), whereas in Extensions 1, 12 and 13, where only shacks are to be found, residents have no electricity. According to our informants in these sections, paraffin and coal, for instance, are the most common means of cooking. Only two clinics service an estimated population of 20 000, resulting in long queues. It's not unusual for people seeking health care to queue as early as four o'clock in the morning. Such is the pressure on this scarce service that by the time the clinic opens at eight o'clock, the queue has to be cut off as only so many people can be seen or treated on any given day.

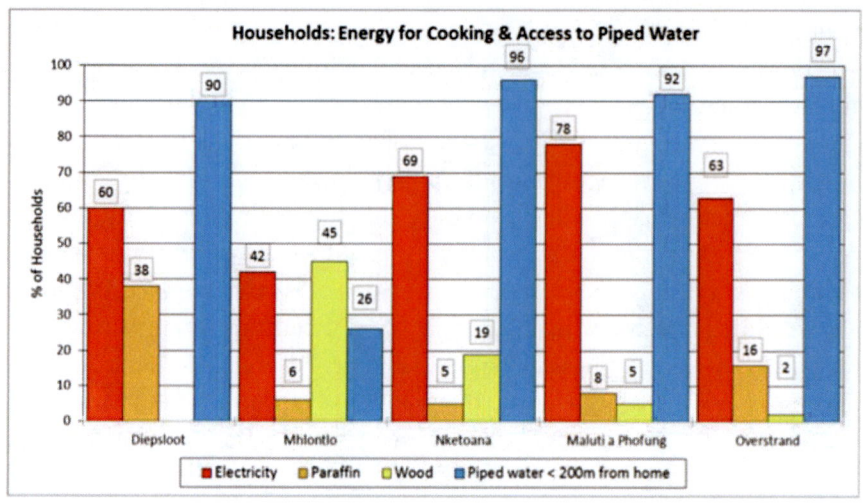

Figure 7: Households Energy for Cooking and Access to Piped Water, Source: Census 2011: Community Profiles in SuperCross, published by Stats SA

These shortcomings, although a major issue in Diepsloot, are not a sign of the lack of State presence, but rather a sign of the strain to meet the extent of the need. And, where the State has failed to provide services, they have been substituted by local initiatives. Not only are the local substitutes filling in a gap, but they are also exploiting the high level of desperation. One such area is policing.

An area that is already tension ridden, characterised by extreme unemployment and experiencing a constant flow of people, Diepsloot is especially prone to criminality. 'We are safe until eight o'clock, and after eight, we are no longer safe because the streets are filled with drunkards and then there are gangsters,' (Focus group interviews: 24–25 November 2012) one resident remarked. This is one area where residents feel the State is failing them. They accuse the police of corruption, ineptitude, and sometimes of being in collusion with criminals.

A young man who ran a *spaza* shop, one respondent informed us, was robbed by a criminal gang known to the community. He followed them clandestinely to their hideout, then called the CPF who promptly alerted the police:

The police then arranged a show-off operation. They brought in some reinforcement and in broad daylight some strange unit in berets swooped on this house. Only one of the reported five gang members was caught.

They didn't make an arrest because four of the criminals were not at the scene (Interview: 11 December 2012).

Later that night the *spaza* shop owner was killed in his shack. At the end of this story the respondent was visibly shaken and his eyes glazed.

Moreover, in 2011 a police captain, one respondent reported, was arrested for extortion. He had rounded up tavern owners who were operating without licences. Having promised the captain the R1,500 'fine', one of the tavern owners reported the captain to the police. A sting operation was arranged with an undercover police and the captain was arrested. Another police officer was arrested while inside the police station, having demanded a R100 bribe to make a docket disappear.

Residents not only lack trust in the police, but also do not take them seriously. One resident explains: '…you see, whenever you report a case they don't take you seriously, and if you are a girl they do. Let's say you are fighting with your boyfriend, you get their attention very quickly. And on the way they are proposing to you' (Focus group interviews: 24–25 November 2012). As a result, residents have devised their own ways of combating crime. One of them is blowing a whistle when suspecting criminal activity or under attack. This alerts the community to come to one's aid. This device is not entirely effective, though. According to one resident: 'sometimes when you blow your whistle, no one comes to help. And sometime when you blow that whistle that person takes note of where the whistle came from and comes to kill you at night…' (ibid.).

Consequently, other residents counsel harsh measures against criminals, which they argue have proved effective elsewhere. That is, if a person is caught by the community for murder, the suspect must also be killed, which is, according to one resident:

…right, because it's me who kills at the end. I go to the police station and I get arrested. I come out after one year. I return and I will kill again and I will kill again and after I have returned I will kill again. I believe if you kill them, they will be scared, truly speaking because you get scared when you steal and see or think you will also be killed (ibid.).

Another crime fighting strategy has been the formation of the Community Police Forum (CPF). The relationship between the Forum and the police, however, explained a local leader, was sour. There appears to be a competition to win the hearts and minds of residents as to who is more effective against criminals in Diepsloot. Most people interviewed expressed a preference or better trust in the CPF, compared to the police, and cite the killing of the *spaza* owner (noted above) as the reason.

The influence of the CPF has consequently made it a target for police control. One senior police official maintained, for instance, that one of his senior colleagues was endearing himself to the youthful section of the Forum, while marginalising the older members. The senior officer, according to the interviewee, hopes that having the Forum on his side would improve his standing within the community and get it to overlook his misdemeanours (Interview: 2012).

Meanwhile, the CPF has been known to lead street patrols. They accost and detain suspects before handing them over to the police. In cases where the suspect has been accused of serious crime such as rape or murder, the CPF has been known to allow angry residents to dispense street justice, which has sometimes led to the killing of such suspects. Again, residents here blame the police. They say the police would arrest a known offender, only for such an offender (often feared in the community) to be released without explanation, and he would in turn intimidate, or in the worst case scenario, kill the person that laid the charge. Overall, residents contend that the CPF is quick and effective in dispensing justice.

Because they provide a valuable service, members of the CPF have become beneficiaries of patronage. Shop owners provide groceries, airtime and other favours to known and influential members of the CPF in return for protection from extortionists, or would-be robbers in their shops.

The South African National Civic Organisation (Sanco) has assumed a similar role. In light of the desperate need for housing, Sanco has been accused of soliciting bribes from desperate home seekers, promising to use their influence to bump them up the waiting list for RDP houses and 'selling' plots of land that do not belong to them. The effect of this, say some of the informants, is that plots originally earmarked for a specific number of households are now being overcrowded as more households are squeezed into the allocated land.

In other words, Sanco has set itself up as an alternative political authority, challenging the legitimate institutions of authority to allocate resources and services. In what seems an attempt to prove that it can do a better job than councillors, the organisation is known for organising popular marches to voice grievances over a range of issues, including service delivery. These

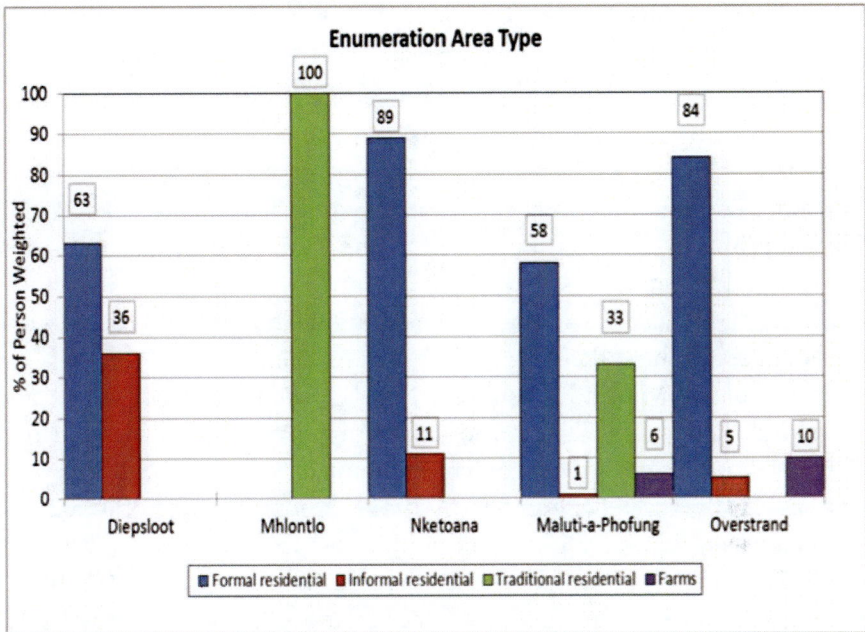

Figure 8: Enumeration Area Type, Source: Census 2011: Community Profiles in SuperCross, published by Stats SA

protests are viewed sceptically by some sections of the Diepsloot community, however. The ANC is particularly dismissive of the declared motives for the protests. One informant said when he arrived in Diepsloot, one of the first things he saw was a march for service delivery, which he joined. 'I was later told the marches organised by Sanco are not in the interest of the community. They are just causing confusion.' (Interview: January 2012.) And the ANC often accuses Sanco of manipulating community members' genuine grievances to advance their own agenda: namely to increase their visibility, portray themselves as active community leaders and thus increase their chances of winning local government elections.

Instances of State weaknesses therefore provide space for the emergence of alternative institutions to provide what are ordinarily State functions and services. But, rather than providing such services as a right to fellow citizens, they do so in return for material gains. It is a source of livelihood encapsulated in a form of patron-client relationship.

RIVALRY AMONG THE LOCAL POLITICAL ELITE

Political office is highly contested among local politicians. The rivalry manifests itself both within party structures as well as in the municipality. Qumbu and Petsana are instructive in this regard.

In both communities, local politicians are pitted against each other. The fight is primarily over positions within the party and in the municipal council. And the squabbles are not only confined within the municipality or local branch, but also cut across the organisational hierarchy to regional and provincial leadership echelons.

In Qumbu's Mhlontlo municipality, a failed attempt to remove Mzimkhulu Jeremiah Jikijela and Mandisa Giyose from the Executive Committee (Exco) of the Municipal Council, bears out the divisions, especially between Jikijela and the regional leadership. The council had passed a resolution removing Jikijela and Giyose from Exco on 20 February 2009, citing poor performance and that they brought the ANC and the municipality into disrepute. Jikijela and Giyose – hereafter referred to as applicants – appealed their removal in court in July 2010, on the grounds that the Exco did not follow proper procedure. The gist of their appeal was that they were not given prior notice that, among the agenda issues, the meeting was to deal with the matter of their removal from the Exco. The council did not contest the procedural requirement of notice, but insisted that it did provide the two applicants with notice that a proposal to remove them was tabled for discussion at the specified meeting.

The court proceedings reveal not only disregard for procedures, but also use of deceitful measures to legitimise impropriety. Before delving into the court details, it is worth noting that the resort to court followed failed appeals to the ANC for intervention. Jikijela and Giyose initially approached the regional leadership, through its secretary, Siyakholwa Mlamli, but the appeal was not concluded. Thereafter, they approached the Provincial Executive Committee, which appointed Xolile Nqatha to investigate. They were never informed of the outcome of the meeting, giving the impression that the investigation simply fizzled out.

Appearing in court as a respondent, the municipal council first disputed the date of the meeting that decided on the removal. Contrary to 20 February 2009 that is cited by the applicants, the municipality insisted that the decision was made at the meeting on 23 March 2009, and that the applicants were advanced a notice of the tabling of their removal on 4 March 2009. Evidence presented in court, however, showed municipal assertions to be false. The notice of the removal was actually dated 16 March 2009 and had not been signed by the municipal manager, Monde Sondaba, as is procedural, but by another. In other words, the notice was generated days after the date claimed by the municipality, and was thus rendered invalid.

On examining the minutes of the meeting convened on 20 February 2009 (which were signed on 9 April 2009 by both the Speaker and the municipal manager) the Judge also discovered that the decision to remove the applicants was actually taken in that meeting, not on 23 March 2009 as claimed by the municipality. Specifically, the minutes note that 'the reshuffling of the Exco is listed…as a motion without notice' and their removal is reflected under Resolution no. 04–20/02/2009 to be effected 'with immediate effect'. Accordingly, the March 2009 salary slips of the applicants showed a deduction that was consistent with loss of additional income, which they had received owing to their service in the Exco. In its defence, the municipality maintained that the minutes were signed by mistake without their being proof-read. The judge expressed his incredulity at the response: '…it is difficult to imagine that two officials who both hold responsible positions can sign a document containing important resolutions of the council without satisfying themselves as to the veracity of the content thereof' (Umthatha High Court Judgement, 2011, p. 12).

The lead up to the 2011 local elections saw yet another round of infighting. This time Jikijela faced up against a local politician and a member of the Hlubi Traditional Council, Mzikalimela Mxinwa. It was over the nomination of the party's candidate for Ward 19. Both vied for the Ward 19 nomination and Mxinwa appeared to have an edge because of his position as chair of the ANC branch in that ward. This was the reason that Jikijela, together with 'drunken-boys'[2], according to Mxinwa, stormed a legitimate Branch General Meeting, held at Mdabukweni village, to nominate the party's candidate. Jikijela claimed that the meeting could not proceed without his permission. A meeting that was subsequently reconvened, Mxinwa further explained, nominated him the party's candidate for Ward 19 (Fieldwork notes: 22–31 May 2012).

Jikijela then convened his own meeting of what he insisted was the legitimate ANC branch in Ward 19. He claimed to be chairperson of that branch. This meant that Ward 19 had two ANC branches, instead of the usual one. Effectively, the local ANC was plunged into what locals have come

---

2. Fieldwork notes: 22–31 May 2012

to call 'parallelism' – multiple organisational structures, each claiming legitimacy and authority. And, Jikijela's branch nominated him candidate, while the other branch nominated Mxinwa.

Mxinwa did not make it onto the final list of candidates. Despite his protest that he had been nominated by a legitimate ANC branch in Ward 19, Jikijela's name was put forward instead. Mxinwa is convinced that the provincial leadership was biased and colluded with Jikijela. This explained, according to Mxinwa, Jikijela's taunts 'that he would die a poor man because he is supported by "small boys" whilst he is supported by the Party's PEC' (Fieldwork notes: 22–31 May 2012.). On close examination, Jikijela's nomination did indicate a relaxation of the party's own policies on the part of the provincial leadership. The ANC had previously resolved to bar their members from holding other employment, whilst serving as councillor. As a principal of Tshilitwa High School, Jikijela did not qualify for nomination, yet he retained his principal post whilst serving as ward councillor.

Jikijela's dual position as principal and councillor makes him an influential figure in Mhlontlo. Mxinwa charges that Jikijela seeks out these positions, specifically for the influence and power that they accord their occupant. According to Mxinwa, this is also what has put him at loggerheads with the Hlubi Traditional Authority: 'He "hijacks" development and wants to take credit for even those things that were organised by the Chief' (ibid.). Jikijela's biography suggests he is relatively more knowledgeable and would have had exposure to influential figures. He worked for the Transkei Department of Foreign Affairs as a Labour representative based in Pretoria and Durban, holds an honours degree in Education Management, and is currently studying towards a Masters degree in Public Administration. He keeps an impressive company crediting Reverend Harris Majeke (current ambassador to India), Mr Stone Sizani (ANC MP), and Mr Mandisi Mpahlwa (former Cabinet Minister) for recruiting him into the ANC.

Jikijela eventually resigned around mid-2012. The ANC eventually forced him to choose between being principal and councillor. He chose the former. His successor was Mawethu Kiviet, who won in an uncontested by-election held on 1 August 2012. Some residents, however, remained unsure whether or not Jikijela was no longer councillor. The confusion stemmed from Jikijela going around telling residents that he was still councillor. This suggests he had resigned reluctantly. Residents seemed unable to independently verify the claim. One resident put it as follows:

Okay, let me raise the truth here, as we were still confused. Mr. Kiviet came and disclosed that he was councillor in our village and I saw him in the office because our councillor used to be Jikijela. So he came to our village to tell us that he is the new councillor. So now some of us do not understand as yet what is going on and I just want us to be on line and not be confused (Focus group interviews: 7–8 December 2012).

These residents were clearly victims of misinformation. They lacked the know-how to determine the truth for themselves. But, even in instances where they suspected the truth, they seemed hesitant to acknowledge that publicly. People seemed fearful to support the 'wrong leader' as councillors could provide a livelihood. 'There are two camps of the ANC here,, one resident explained:

If you are not following this particular one or you do not attend meetings it becomes clear when you are really poor. Could that be true because when you really need a job they will tell you that we do not know this one, he is not one of us, so I want to know if that is true from the government? (ibid.).

Other residents still follow 'the old councillor while we have the new one now'. The cause of all this, he explained, is 'poverty, because a person follows the side that will bring food on the table. But, the first one did not do anything for us and we cannot blame the new one as yet' (ibid.). Thus residents complain bitterly of favouritism. Some get employment in public works projects or food parcels, whilst others are excluded:

…there are things that do not go well from the people that we have elected as our leaders like things like tractors by the councillors. We hear of things that are supposed to come our way but you will find that there is discrimination and things do not really come to the satisfaction of the people. You will notice that the government has given us tractors but they end up being given to people who live closer to the councillor. The government does provide for us, but the councillor favours people that live closer to him. All this goes back to the issue of service delivery because we see development in other parts of the wards like some people have toilets built for them, but not for everybody (ibid.).

Councillors, our respondents informed us, even go to great lengths to deny other residents opportunities. A public meeting, for instance, would not start if the unwanted persons are in attendance or the favourites are absent. Politicians employ all manner of trickery to either get the *persona non grata* to leave, or delay commencing a meeting until their intended beneficiaries have arrived. One resident explained it as follows:

> *...I also stopped attending meetings. It happens that we are called for a meeting in a certain place like he says there are two camps, we go to the meeting and sit there with no one present to host the meeting and you find that they are phoning each other and telling people not to come to the meeting and people end up leaving and when they realise that we have left they come to the meeting, in so much that there are meetings that take place in the evenings because of such things* (Focus group interviews: 7–8 December 2012).

If not convened under false pretences, or to dispense patronage to supporters, meetings are used to dupe illiterate locals into signing forms to nominate candidates for local elections. Such shenanigans are what got one resident to stop attending public meetings:

> *...people will be told to bring IDs because there are job opportunities, and people would do so and they would fill in some forms only to find that the forms are for voting for a certain individual and not a job opportunity. So people have been discouraged by such things because they heard about; yes, meetings are called but people do not have trust anymore and it is because of them* (ibid.).

Diepsloot residents, too, complained of self-serving politicians and factionalism. People are deceived into joining the party with the promise of a job or other sorts of favours: 'They say we must register. We pay R48 for membership that they say is valid for four years. But that membership (card) will only come when one finishes the term and someone new starts, and when it comes, it has already expired ... okay' (ibid.). In the meantime, other people have got the spoils:

> *You go there, you attend meetings, but when things start happening, there are people ... you'd find that there are people who are here and*

there, they are jacks of all trades, there are women here in Diepsloot who are known as Ms so and so, you end up a nobody, they use us to progress, but they are the ones who are gaining something.

Membership of ANC, they tell us that when things happen we will be a part of it, they use us (Focus group interviews: 24–25 November 2012).

Samuel Seale, an ANC activist, added further details charging Councillor Makhubela with employing card carrying members in community development projects. The idea, according Seale, is that beneficiaries of employment, in turn, vote for him in the contest for the nomination as the party's candidate in local government elections. Seale had lost out to Makhubela in the contest for the party's nominee for the 2011 local elections, a loss he ascribed to Makhubela's supply of patronage to members of the party in his branch. But, Seale was not the only person who had made this claim, several other people interviewed, including those who were not leading any of the many local forums or organisations in Diepsloot, had complained about this, corroborating Seale's charge (Fieldwork notes: 23 July 23).

The same complaint of favouritism and exclusion in employment was echoed in Free State's Petsana as well. It came up in two budget forum meetings held in May 2012 at Kgotso/Uxolo High School and KwaThabileng Guest Lodge, which were observed in the course of fieldwork. At the former meeting for instance, Phindi Zwane, an unemployed youth serving in the Ward 9 Committee, complained that some people were excluded from employment in one chicken slaughter project, which is implemented by a local company, VKB Company. Though called to finalise the budget proposal, the discussions quickly turned towards how people were hired on local development projects and why others were not given opportunities (Fieldwork notes: 18–25 May 2012).

The audience became even more agitated because the mayor could not even account for how the budget of the previous year was spent. There was no report at the meeting on what the municipality had achieved with last year's budget. The problem seemed to be that the mayor, who was meant to avail the annual report at the end of the last financial year, had not done so. This left people at the meeting in the dark. But the mayor and municipal officials insisted that people take them at their word, that they had made some improvements with last year's budget allocation. In the absence of visible improvements, however, the attendees doubted the assurances. According to one of them, a young person representing the youth, Phindi Zwane, the mayor was simply staging a charade of public participation just to get the community to rubberstamp the budget. Thereafter, she would go on to utilise the budget allocation as she saw fit. To Phindi: 'There is no real accountability in Petsana municipality' (Fieldwork notes: 18–25 May 2012).

As the crowd found the mayor's answers unsatisfactory, the mayor began to lose control of the meeting. The meeting broke into near pandemonium. More than half of the attendees walked out before the end of the meeting. Ultimately, not much was discussed about the budget, which was supposed to be the core issue on the agenda.

The mayor ascribed the tension at the meeting to irregular contact. More public meetings, she reckoned, would ensure that people were kept abreast of municipal activities and performance. This is why, the mayor expanded, she failed to connect with the crowd. For an observer, however, the mayor was not just failing to connect, but she simply was not able to articulate whatever she might have had in mind. Her colleagues, a councillor in one instance, and a municipal official in another, had to intervene and articulate what they guessed she was trying to communicate.

It was evident that councillors lacked confidence in the mayor and her municipal manager. They even staged a protest in February 2012, storming the manager's office, for which they were arrested. They were charged with trespassing, acts of violence, and intimidation against the administrative staff in the municipality offices. The charges were laid by the municipal manager, effectively against the entire municipal council (Field notes: 16–23 February 2012).

Views on the cause of the confrontation vary, however. Mme Palesa, a former councillor during the previous municipal term and currently a teacher, ascribes the tension to councillors' frustration with what they perceive to be indifference on the part of the municipal administration[3] towards service delivery. The reality, according to Mme Palesa, who declined nomination in line with ANC policy against multiple jobs, is that councillors over promised voters service delivery without considering whether or not resources were available and that their time-frames were realistic (ibid.).

A member of the executive committee of the local ANC branch, Mme Palesa believes the stalemate shows that councillors do not understand their

---

3. She opted to keep her teaching job because she considers a political career unstable. There was no guarantee that she would be nominated for the next elections, while her teaching qualifications guarantee her a relatively secure employment.

council role and their indivdual responsibilities as councillors. For Mme Palesa there has never been sufficient induction of councillors prior to taking over their responsibilities. In her experience as a councillor, her council avoided unnecessary tension with the municipal manager's office and that helped in the implementation of programmes.

Conversely, Councillor Semela believes that the stalemate happened precisely because they are doing their job. Semela, who stays in a backyard 'shack' at his mother's house, was one of the councillors arrested. He boasted that 'we are the first council to truly stand with the community. We will never fall because we identify with our community' (Fieldwork notes: 16–23 February 2012). The previous Council, Semela charged, was in cahoots with the municipal management and had been compromised when it came to taking the grievances of the community forward. Semela and his colleagues found it unacceptable that they had been in office for a period of seven months and yet they could not point to any new thing done. Instead, they allege, the municipal manager is more interested in awarding residential sites to people who support him.

A municipal official, Fikile, was puzzled by the discontent. To her the new municipal council was a great improvement from the previous one: 'We have had the first unqualified audit, and we emerge from disclaimer, then qualified, so we have achieved a lot'. The main problem she identified was that councillors have not been supportive of the municipal officials and they do not acknowledge the success by officials (Fieldwork notes: 18–25 May 2012).

Fikile did, however, hint that the council could not do much in terms of social development. The budget does not quite allow for it. Not many people pay rates. Municipal coffers therefore are slim. The indigent policy, which provides a certain quota of free water and electricity to low income earners, is the best they can do.

Another interview with a group of women who had gathered at Mme Pontsho's home in Ward 8, revealed yet another interesting insight into the impasse. The women had gathered to discuss initiatives that would earn them a living. They were highly dismissive of the present council. The municipality, they contended, is not useful in assisting to implement poverty alleviation programmes and working with women, such as Mme Pontsho, who is responsible for registration of co-operatives in the area. They charge that councillors want their people in the management of the municipality, including in the position of municipal manager. The latter comes from Parys, which has engendered a popular refrain: 'Everything is decided in Parys', (the home town of the premier of the province, Ace Magashule). Previously, the municipal manager was a local, but according to the women, that did not make him any better, as 'the manager was corrupt and he hired his close relatives to key positions in the municipality'. They consider the current manager an improvement on his predecessor (Fieldwork notes: 18–25 May 2012).

For one of the women, Mme Puleng, the young ANC councillors are just insolent and disrespectful towards elders. Because she could not tolerate rude behaviour from the young councillor, she opted to vote for a DA candidate, who is now a councillor in her ward.

Moreover, Mme Puleng explained that she voted for the DA so that it could 'fix a few things', and then she would vote back an ANC councillor. In face of a barrage of criticism from her colleagues over her vote for the DA, she insisted that she is still an ANC member, but wanted to get things done (Fieldwork notes: 18–25 May 2012).

Councillors in Petsana have no confidence in the mayor. The idea that the mayor is a Proportional Representation (PR) councillor has also been alluded to, to demonstrate that she is controlled by party structure/leadership at provincial level. As a PR councillor, she is seen as weak and could be dismissed easily. When PR councillors are dismissed, no by-elections are held. A party simply makes a replacement. A dismissal of a ward councillor, however, results in by-elections, which introduces the possibility of a loss – something parties are not keen to risk.

Lack of employment generates tremendous expectations on the municipality to create jobs. Consequently, councillors see job creation as a pivotal part of their duty. Municipal officials, however, disagree. At the Budget Forum meeting, held at Petsana's KwaThabileng Guest Lodge, for instance, Stephanie Venter, a municipal official responsible for the IDP, urged councillors to desist from making promises to create jobs (ibid.). Thus, councillors see providing livelihood (job creation) as a pivotal part of their job and their electoral mandate. They provide means of livelihood and assist locals either to gain access to employment elsewhere or to some form of services.

In Diepsloot, for instance, a substantial number of residents visiting the councillor's office come to secure a form called: 'Proof of Residence'. This document is the most valued piece of paper for most of Diepsloot residents, particularly those who reside in informal sections or rented shacks in the backyards of formal houses. Councillor Makhubela explained that with fraud so rampant, banking institutions, employers, and retail shops were reluctant to enter into any agreement with individuals when they could not produce a proof of residence. The form, signed by the councillor, vouches for the local residence of the bearer. It reflects the bearer's ID number, address (that is, the stand number), and the extension where the stand is to be found.

The municipal manager seems to wield more power than the mayor due to protection from the provincial leadership. The use of Operation Hlasela, a provincial government programme ostensibly to address problems related to service delivery, has also come to light. The programme has been criticised as a vehicle for corruption. However, some have given it good reviews and have noted how it undercuts the bureaucratic requirement of government before intervention can take place. The remarks are that, 'with operation Hlasela you get a problem solved now, you get hired on the spot'. What does this mean? This lends itself to interpretations that Hlasela can be used to dispense patronage, buying leaders popularity as they are seen to act instantaneously. This approach may raise concern that Hlasela is not implemented fairly and openly.

With other opportunities of employment absent, locals have come to expect municipalities to assume a central role in creating employment. This has placed municipalities and councillors at the centre of job creation initiatives in the local economy. Beyond simply meeting a dire need for a livelihood, councillors use job opportunities as a way of boosting their own electoral fortunes in contests within the party. This has placed them on opposing ends with the municipal officials. The latter sees job creating simply as a consequence of their primary role of providing social services to their communities.

Competition between parties also generates its own dynamic in terms of promises that are made to secure votes and methods used to retain them. Besides promises of jobs, services, and social grants, parties use their varied access to private and public resources to advance their interests – ranging from food parcels to blankets and clothes. In some instances, parties do resort to divisive and sometimes racist tactics. A case in point is SMSs that were purportedly circulated by a DA councillor in the Overberg District. The one SMS read: '*Botrivier anargiste oorgehaal om te vernietig, vrees en paniek te saai. Dink nie wat dit aan ons gemeenskap doen nie. DA sal beskerm wat hulle vernietig!*' (Botriver anarchists [persuaded and convinced] ready to fight and destroy, to spread fear and panic. Think what it will do to your community. The DA will protect what they destroy!) And another SMS warned residents 'that Africans were going to burn down the schools and instigate racial conflict' (Community Workshop: Grabouw Country Club, 18 July 2012). The SMSs stoked racial tension between Africans and Coloureds in a community that had previously been characterised by relatively peaceful racial relations.

The aforementioned findings demonstrate a strong correlation between economic status and patronage politics. Both indigent and affluent residents use the local State apparatus in a variety of ways to secure patronage. Similarly, the local politicians dispense patronage for self enrichment, and to gain political support. In some instances, State weaknesses have created a vacuum for local 'strongmen' who have emerged to serve as patrons, fulfilling what is ordinarily the role of the State in exchange for an income. This exerts a deleterious impact on the meaning of politics, public participation in political life and institutions, competence and public trust in public institutions, and cohesiveness of local communities.

CHAPTER 5

ANALYSIS & CONCLUSION

This research study examines patronage politics in contemporary South Africa at the local interface of the citizens and the State. Specifically, the case studies sought to determine the nature of patronage politics, identify factors that promote this phenomenon, and establish its impact on local politics. This chapter analyses the implication of the findings, in relation to the said primary question of the study, and concludes the report.

Before delving into analysis, suffice to note that the study was not without assumptions of its own. It assumes that patronage politics does thrive under conditions of poverty and inequality. Though not entirely accurate, poverty is especially singled out in some literature as a dominant cause of patronage politics. It is argued that, because they are poor and face an uncertain future due to the lack of professional qualifications, both voters and politicians seek out and benefit from patronage. Politicians do so through their control over political power in unscrupulous ways, while voters cast their votes for a particular party in return for material gains. Voters are dependent on the State. This implies that politics is reduced strictly to the use of political power, not to fashion society along a particular set of ideas, but largely to fulfil material wants – many of which are dispensed to specific individuals or groups in return for their political support. This assumption is made not to preclude the prevalence of patronage in more affluent settings, but with the aim of understanding the bi-directional relationship between poverty (and inequality) and patronage in the specific circumstances that were examined.

In undertaking the research, we adopted a case study approach, setting the study within five local communities (or municipalities). This approach not only allows for a variety of research techniques, such as interviews and participant observation, but also affords researchers a reasonable period of time to gather meaningful data. The subject of patronage politics is a sensitive one as it involves, among other things, pointing fingers at people who are possibly corrupt, and by doing so placing one's safety or livelihood at risk. Potential interviewees do not open up easily for interviews with strangers. The researchers in this study had thus to gain the trust of respondents first, something that was partly secured by assurance of anonymity. As such, in most instances pseudonyms are used for the subjects who are directly quoted or referred to. Where real names are used, this is with the consent of the individuals concerned. Gaining trust requires frequent and longer visits to the community and thus researchers visited the communities over a period of eight months. They interviewed individuals and groups, and attended meetings and social or recreational activities. In addition to individual and groups interviews, the findings of the study also drew from interviews with 20 focus groups selected from each of the five research sites.

The communities selected for the study varied from an informal settlement in Johannesburg, a fishing community along the east coast of the Western Cape province, to a township in the rural town of the Free State province, and a village in Qumbu, part of the former Transkei bantustan. The multiplicity of case studies affords insight into how patronage politics pans out in different communities, characterised by varying histories, institutions, age of communities, and profiles of inhabitants.

The research findings confirm some of the assertions in the literature, while challenging others. Equally important to note is that the findings not only shed light on our case studies, but also apply to other municipalities throughout the country. This is borne out by official and empirical reports (the Auditor General's office and official ANC reports), which are cited below, that not only validate these findings, but also demonstrate the ubiquitous nature of these dynamics. Accordingly, while the conclusions derive from the particular case studies an attempt is made to generalise them to other municipalities.

POVERTY AND UNEMPLOYMENT INDUCES DEPENDENCE ON THE STATE

The State plays a pivotal role in the lives of the unemployed and indigent. Because they lack a source of livelihood, the State has come to provide for their subsistence. Social relief takes multiple forms, ranging from cash transfers to food parcels and lighting material, such as paraffin and electricity, and water. Social grants support some 40% of South African households, without which they would live in abject poverty.

Official relief extends to providing employment in public works. Though short-term, public works employment is highly coveted by locals. Employment is scarce, given the high national official rate of unemployment of which roughly 25%, broadly defined, goes into the mid-30s in percentage terms. This triggers intense competition among locals for the few, temporary jobs available. Tension has consequently arisen, especially in instances where locals feel that 'others' such as residents from outside their community and foreign-born residents, are preferred over them for employment, or are able to thrive better than the 'locals' in small business activity. In places such as Diepsloot, the tension has previously imploded into full-blown violence against foreign nationals. Such is the level of desperation to secure employment.

Reliance on social and other forms of relief, in turn, makes the State's provision of official documents, such as IDs, especially critical for the indigent. Unlike other citizens not dependent on social grants, recipients of grants depend on IDs not only to apply for the grants, but also to access them on a monthly basis. This documentation is their gateway to subsistence. One young man, Skhumbuzo Mhlongo, in 2009 committed suicide in anger after an official at Pinetown's Home Affairs tore up his ID application. The young man, whose parents had died, needed to provide supporting accounts that he was South African-born. The official did not believe the accounts, meaning that Mhlongo would be without an ID, making it difficult for him to access any form of livelihood. He chose death (http://news24.com).

Equally noteworthy is that it is not sufficient that such services are available in the vicinity; rather they should be located within their *residential* area. Proximity is critical for poor people to access official services. Distance oftentimes requires the use of public transportation. This requires money they do not have. Equally important is the use of media to communicate availability and location of such opportunities. Media reaches not only a wider audience, but is quite crucial for those who are illiterate and is even best in their mother tongue. It appears that the State does make optimal use of radio to announce services and programmes – but given migration and reception in various parts of the country, as illustrated in the case of Overstrand, this does not reach all the intended targets.

For residents of informal settlements, such as part of Diepsloot, the reliance on officialdom stretches beyond the ordinary. Because shacks do not have a documented formal address, informal dwellers lack official documentation that verifies their residence. This presents a problem in their interactions with officialdom. They need proof of residence. Councillors provide such proof. This increases residents' dependence on the State even more and makes them vulnerable in the presence of unscrupulous officials.

It is important to note, however, that the dependence is reciprocal. Councillors need the votes of the poor to remain in office. This requires that councillors attend to their needs. That they do not always perform these duties diligently notwithstanding, councillors are acutely conscious that their political fate depends on meeting the needs of their poor constituency.

Councillors' dependence on votes, in turn, gives residents leverage. They are buoyed to make demands upon their public representatives. Indifference to such demands risks loss of political support. Consequently, councillors take great effort to provide patronage, as noted in the case of Mhlontlo and Diepsloot, going beyond what is ordinarily prescribed in their duties. This patron-client relationship was confirmed by an ANC task team, formed in 2011 to investigate party squabbles over local government nominations: 'During the investigation, it became clear that most ANC branches are run by unemployed members who look up to ward councillors for employment as in many municipalities there are few or no economic opportunities for the unemployed members' (ANC, 2012, p. 13).

In the other words, patron-client relations are beneficial to both parties. Councillors are guaranteed political support, especially within party contests over nominations, and supporters secure the much-needed material benefits. Albeit mutually beneficial to the two parties, such relations erode meritocracy in employment recruitment. Rather, it puts a premium on personal or political relations above anything else. Securing a job depends on who one knows, rather than one's competence.

Consequently, residents have come to rely strongly on nepotism. By nepotism in this case, and as used in popular lexicon, we not only mean granting favours or preference to family members, but also to friends and political allies: Applying for a job and submitting a curriculum vitae seems to have become inconsequential. As a result, residents have come to accept, and are resigned to, such practices. It has become the way of life, about which residents feel nothing can be done. Those without relatives or friends in places of employment appear more likely to remain unemployed. Personal ties (or primordial identities) therefore have become extremely important as a way of securing a livelihood.

Put differently, people are taking 'care of their own'. This is especially salient in the areas of Overstrand that are somewhat diverse and have relatively large 'migrant' communities. This accentuates ethnic identities and the result is tension, as an ethnic group feels marginalised in favour of another.

POLITICAL OFFICE AS SOURCE OF EMPLOYMENT – POWER STRUGGLES

Recipients of social grants, however, are not the only citizens dependent on the State for a livelihood. Local politicians, too, are dependent on political office for an income. Without a political office, a sizeable number are likely to battle to secure employment. Though Mhlontlo's Jeremiah Jikijela and Petsana's Mme Bongi hold professional qualifications, a significant number of councillors are without them – like councillor Semela who lives in the back room at his parents' house.

A study administered by the Local Government Sector for Education and Training (LGSETA), among newly elected councillors in 2011 for instance, is quite revealing in this regard. The councillors had attended an induction programme, part of which was to determine their qualifications and training needs. Of the total 8,398 that took part in the programme, 4,037 answered the questionnaire, representing 40% of the total number of participants (LGSETA, 2011).

The results of the questionnaire revealed that more than a quarter of the sample had not completed primary or secondary schooling, and less than a quarter managed to complete matric. Those with tertiary and post-graduate qualification made up the smallest component of the sample. Given the scarcity of labour-intensive employment and their lack of formal qualifications, political office is pretty much the only source of income for such politicians.

This would explain why political office is so highly contested among local politicians. Candidates, as in the case of Mhlontlo's Jikijela and Mxinwa, employ unscrupulous ways to secure both a party nomination and, once elected, re-nomination. In a party nomination contest, residents, especially those who are illiterate, such as the villagers of Mhlontlo, are made to sign forms under false pretences of applying for jobs. This is how a parallel party branch in Mhlontlo's Ward 19 appears to have been formed. Residents were duped and the wily politician was able to sign up members in support of his party's nomination for the 2011 local elections.

Controversy over nominations, especially for the 2011 local elections, however, was not confined to Mhlontlo; it was commonplace and widespread throughout the country. A subsequent task team set up by the ANC to investigate the complaints (for instance) registered its concern:

It is worth noting that during the election processes almost every province had experienced violent protests and growing intolerance emanating from, among others, dissatisfaction with the nomination and selection of candidate processes, albeit to varying degrees. This is indeed a serious matter that would require earnest redress (ANC, 2012, p. 4).

The task team had begun its investigation a month after the local elections held in June 2011. It uncovered all manner of malpractices. Senior leaders deployed to oversee the nomination process at the branch level either turned a blind eye to manipulative practices or sided with one faction against another. In order to secure nomination of a certain individual for instance, members that are known to support a rival candidate would not be allowed into a meeting, even though they had valid membership cards. They would simply be told that they were not on 'The Wisdom List'. In some cases, names of nominees would simply be removed and substituted with names of favourite individuals. This meant disregarding choices made by branches and endorsed by the public through public participation processes. Some of the candidates 'only joined the ANC after being nominated. In certain instances the candidates (now incumbent councillors) have shockingly little knowledge of the ANC' (ANC, 2012, p. 20).

Overall, 419 wards were investigated. Of that number, the task team recommended that 125 wards needed to redo their nominations and, where necessary, election of councillors; this meant that if the disputed councillor was not nominated in the rerun process, he or she would step down. A by-election would then be held. The severity of the manipulations, the task team felt, was such that the organisation should consider instituting criminal charges against the some of the candidates.

The Jikijela-Mxinwa dispute, therefore, was far from unique. The Eastern Cape had the highest number of disputes (167), with the majority coming from the OR Tambo (where Mhlontlo is located) and Amathole regions. In the case of OR Tambo, the report of the Dlamini-Zuma task team, among other things, said:

Worth noting in OR Tambo was the high tension between the Region and the Province as it relates to the list and organisational processes. Consequently, in OR Tambo in particular, some list processes were sanctioned by the REC; while others were conducted by resident PEC members without the knowledge and mandate of the REC.

> *Almost all the disputes from OR Tambo appeared to relate to the changes made by the PEC of the candidates who emerged as the preferred ones from the BGMs conducted by the persons deployed by the Regional Office. These candidates were often replaced with persons who emerged from subsequent processes conducted by resident PEC members* (ANC, 2012, p. 10–11).

The manner in which party members contest nomination not only engenders violation of organisational procedures, but also encourages misuse of state resources. Because nominations depend on securing sufficient votes at a branch level, incumbents build such support through providing employment to some residents, who are also card-carrying party members, to the exclusion of others. In some instances, money is disbursed to branch members as an enticement to vote in particular ways – reflecting an even more extreme manifestation of intra-party patronage and the forging of sinister mutual dependencies.

In Diepsloot, defeated candidates felt that their rivals won unfairly. Mhlontlo's experience tells that the discord extends to the community as a whole. The community becomes divided between winners and losers. When it comes to local employment and other benefits those who ensured a candidate's success are favoured by the victorious candidates (where councillors have discretionary powers).

In other words, rather than create a common platform where residents deliberate and take collective decisions over affairs of their community, politics has become a corrupting influence. It divides the community, instead of uniting it. A sense of community and public participation is consequently waning. Mhlontlo residents expressed disinterest in community meetings because of their exclusive character. They had attended what were supposedly public meetings only to be made to feel unwelcome. Some have opted not to attend public meetings anymore.

Disengagement and weakening of community ties, however, have not quite translated to fatalism. Residents have not entirely resigned themselves to a sense of hopelessness. They have developed alternative ways quite different to the factionalist manner of councillors. And Mhlontlo's Hlubi traditional authority is one example of this. In instances where paid community work goes through the traditional authority, the chief applies a different formula of employing people. Rather than give to supporters of a councillor to the exclusion of others, the authority, together with residents, gives preference to those most in need. This is in keeping with the idea that a traditional authority is the representative of all in the community, regardless of political affiliations or differences, which, after all, is meant to be the guiding principle of public office. As such, the democratic local government system, which is meant to be the representative of the popular will, is delegitimised by manifestations of crass patronage.

But, where councillors use job-creation as patronage, they have also been pitted against municipal officials. Councillors meddle in municipal work, insisting on the delivery of jobs and specific allocations of tenders. Municipal officials do not always co-operate, for job creation is not considered a function of councillors. Officials also have to follow the prescripts of public finance management legislation. This leads to tension, which at times breaks into full-blown confrontation between councillors and municipal officials, such as in the case of Petsana, where the municipal council was consequently thrown into disarray. In such instances, delivery of social services comes to a halt as the municipal council, due to internal squabbles, fails to meet and approve programmes for execution by municipal officials.

Delivery of social services is not the only casualty of the power struggles. Procedures also suffer. Take the case of Mhlontlo's Jeremiah Jikijela. He was re-elected ward councillor of Ward 19 in the 2011 local elections despite his party having decided against councillors holding another job. Though Jikijela eventually resigned a year later, his very nomination suggests laxity of rules. As noted earlier, this is borne out in the report of the Dlamini-Zuma task team.

Relaxation of rules, in turn, reflects on the institution of the party itself. Jikijela's flouting of his party's rules on nomination is not the only symptom of a weak institution. He was nominated by a reportedly illegitimate branch, which he formed because the legitimate branch would not nominate him. Jikijela would not accede to the decision of the legitimate branch, which had nominated his rival, Mxinwa. The provincial leadership of the party, despite protestations, did not disqualify Jikijela, but instead approved his nomination. Institutional rules were subverted in favour of a personality. As noted earlier, this had a lot do with factionalism that afflicts party structures.

The subversion of rules is not confined to parties alone. Rather, it is also practiced within official institutions and involves many other officials. The failed attempt to remove Jikijela from the Executive Committee (Exco) of the Municipal Council is indicative of the ends to which rivals are willing to go and the nature of tactics they employ in their power struggles. Jikijela's rivals in the council, as the court proceedings revealed, falsified, manipulated and fabricated evidence, all in an attempt to remove him.

Such prevalence of institutional violations is inevitable. Once employed within a party, these practices assume a life of their own. Political parties are incubators of political and institutional culture that is consonant with democratic institutions. If one disrespects democratic processes within a political party, the party leadership should communicate its disapproval. For all institutions, including democratic political parties and democratic governing structures, operate on similar principles and spirit. Both have similar expectations of their members and office-bearers. If one thwarts and defies procedures of a political party, there is no stopping that individual from replicating a similar corrosive behaviour within a municipality. In violating the integrity of democratic processes, the transgressor has shown to have an anti-institutional culture. Once developed, that culture applies in a non-discriminatory manner.

It should be of concern that Jikijela is not any other ordinary person. As a school principal, he enjoys an elevated social standing in the village. This explains his acquaintance with highly placed individuals. And furthermore, Jikijela seemed to have basked in the glory of Ward 19 being selected for a presidential rural development project in 2011. It is quite possible that he had nothing to do with this development, but that did not stop him claiming it.

Those without the opportunities open to Jikilela are very insecure because occupation of political office depends on a party nomination. Councillors serve only a five-year term and are not guaranteed re-nomination. This generates a propensity to 'build a nest' in case they are not returned. And because most lack professional qualifications, finding a source of income outside of political office becomes a great cause of anxiety. Thus accusations of councillors influencing decisions over who gets a contract are commonplace. Councillors, in return, get a certain share of the total value of the contract.

At the one level, business people interested in such opportunities put a high premium on having 'dependable' councillors or municipal officials who can push such opportunities their way. These range from catering to local infrastructure projects. Such self-interest infects the party nomination processes and the 'deployment' of council officials.

At another level, councillors award themselves contracts or do so through family members. In the recently released 2011–2012 audit report, the Office of the Auditor General notes that, in 60 municipal entities, councillors (and officials) were found to have been illegally awarded contracts totalling R118 million. Thirty-six of them had committed the same offence before. In another instance, contracts to the value of R104 million, involving 34 of those audited (employees and councillors) did not declare a conflict of interest. Contracts to the value of R93 million were awarded to close family members of councillors and officials. This was discovered in 70 municipal entities of which 7 were repeat offenders. It is not unlawful for family members to do business with municipal auditees.[1] What is troublesome, though, is that suppliers and officials have not declared the relationship, which suggests deliberate concealment that may imply intent to manipulate the process (Office of Auditor-General, 2013).

If not for a mere income, the political rivalry amongst the local elites is therefore spurred by spoils of office. Municipal contracts are one such spoil. This is not only a violation of procedures, but also exerts a deleterious effect on the quality of services delivered by the municipality. Oftentimes work is left incomplete because the budget ran out; the quality of the work is poor (due to contractors being inexperienced or to insufficient building material being used as contractors seek to maximise their profit margin); or council overspends on the original budget as it tries to repair the initial flop.

---

1. All municipal entities.

SELF-INITIATIVE & OFFICIAL ASSISTANCE

High unemployment levels have resulted in some locals initiating activities to generate a living. These vary from formal trades, such as shop owners, who run what are known as spaza shops, to informal traders who sell foodstuffs on the side of the road. Challenges faced by both formal and informal traders call into the question the effectiveness of the State in assisting local economic activities.

In some areas spaza shop owners face stiff competition from shops owned by foreign-born residents. The edge enjoyed by the migrant traders goes beyond longer opening hours, but also extends to the pricing of foodstuffs. They sell at a much cheaper price than locals. This phenomenon is not only confined to Diepsloot. A number of townships throughout South Africa have seen a proliferation of shops owned by foreign-born residents, while local traders seem to have been driven out of business.

In a series of events reported throughout the country, local traders have retaliated with violent attacks on foreign nationals and their properties. In a free market economy, especially if foreign-born shop owners acquire their stock fairly, it is not clear how driving them out benefits the poor consumers. Empirical evidence, including from these case studies, points to the organisation of foreign shop owners into effective bulk buying syndicates, which – on the basis of economies of scale – helps to drive prices down. Should government take it upon itself to assist local traders in this regard, or should this be left to the local business associations, in the spirit of free enterprise? Would such action by government constitute discrimination and further entrench divisions within communities?

Some locals rent out their properties to foreign-born traders to use as shops, while they move out to stay elsewhere. In other words, locals have not been affected similarly by the presence of foreign-born traders. They are a threat to some and a source of income and cheap goods to others. Thus attacks on foreign-born traders are not always spurred by xenophobia. They seem, largely, to manifest intra-class rivalry.

Informal traders, too, face challenges. But theirs are of a different nature and come from a different source. Though helpful in some respects, state assistance seems somewhat inadequate in other respects. Municipalities provide shelters to hawkers under which they can set up their stalls and be protected from bad weather but the way in which municipalities function with respect to informal trade can also be obstructive. Informal traders put up stalls where their customers are concentrated, which is oftentimes on the side of the road. As a result, they come into conflict with overly rigid bylaws. More often than not they are forced off the most convenient spots.

To be sure, the State has introduced measures to offset inconveniences to informal traders. These include locating them within certain premises or requiring that they get permits and are assigned to particular spots on which to sell. Traders are sceptical about the efficiency of such regulations. Zoned areas can only accommodate a certain number of informal traders, and hawkers prefer the flexibility to follow their customers, wherever they may be. The location of customers will generally change from one place to another, especially if, for instance, traders are catering for workers on construction sites. Workers move upon completion of the construction and a new construction elsewhere provides another site for trading. This demands flexibility on the part of the hawkers, and in effect, the municipality. Albeit they are meant to assist, municipal bylaws require an appraisal. Evidence shows that they have become more of a hindrance than an aid.

Informal traders, especially those who aspire to start small businesses, clamour for financial assistance to start relatively bigger operations such as sewing companies. The only lenders they know are the *mashonisas*, or loan sharks, whose interest payments on a loan are much higher than that of financial institutions and are known to employ extra-judicial measures when people default on payment.[2]

Co-operatives at Petsana certainly have nothing positive to report on their interactions with the local municipality. Yet residents were encouraged to form co-operatives with the aim of promoting local economic development. The encouragement seems not to have been followed up by state support or by the setting up of appropriate institutional infrastructure. The local economic development office, for instance, was only opened in Petsana in 2011. Where contracts were issued to locals, they seem to have favoured particular individuals over others – again an instance of patronage, defeating the evidently noble intentions of policy.

---

2. The banking system in South Africa currently keeps unconventional entrepreneurs (such as hawkers and informal traders) out, with no access to credit provided. Furthermore, the National Credit Act is another area of constraint as it places a large emphasis on tangible assets, which automatically eliminates the unconventional entrepreneur. MISTRA is currently working on research that looks at the credit market and its contribution to the low savings rate in the country. The project entitled *The Arithmetic of Savings* will be available in early 2014.

Official Approach to Local Economic Development

Though employment may be scarce, some communities are endowed with natural resources that can be exploited to provide economic opportunities. Mhlontlo and Overstrand municipalities are certainly amongst such communities. One has an abundance of communal land and the other has fish in the ocean. These natural resources are not only a source of subsistence, but also of commercial activity.

Subsistence seems to take precedence in Mhlontlo over commercial activity. There are hardly any co-operatives or developmental projects to encourage commercial activity. Instead, some assistance, such as providing tractors, is made available towards helping locals till the soil. Conversely, Overstrand uses its access to the ocean to promote both commercial activity and subsistence. The way the municipality does this, however, appears to foster inequality among its racially divided residents. Most of Overstrand's poor residents are largely involved in subsistence fishing, whilst the industry itself seems to be dominated by established business.

The dichotomy – black subsistence and mainly white commercial activity – is partly a result of unequal resources. Even though local fishers obtain licence to fish, they still have to rent the facilities – boats and transportation – owned by established entities. All told, they are left with very little of their proceeds which are sufficient only for subsistence. They are unable to accumulate income in order to acquire a boat and other such capital, which would make them self-sufficient. Rather, they fish to live and remain on the economic margin. Access to the ocean is critical to the extent that it should be able to sustain livelihoods, while enabling the generation of meaningful income.

Petsana's experience further accentuates the inadequacy of officialdom towards promoting small business or the informal sector. The numerous co-operatives in Petsana have largely gone unsupported by local government. This is despite official urgings to form co-operatives in order to qualify for government contracts towards local economic development.

There is clearly a keen desire and initiative amongst the poor to lift themselves out of poverty. They are not content living off the largesse of the State. They would rather be self-sufficient, generating their own income. The informal sector already employs a significant number of abled-bodied individuals, estimated around 1.6 million citizens. And it would appear that there is potential for further absorption. Diepsloot's informal traders, for instance, exuded enthusiasm and had many ideas about business and how the State could assist them with start-up capital. But, rather than engage them, the State has tended to criminalise informal traders. They are seen as a problem that requires controlling through all sorts of regulations and licenses. Their economic activities are deemed the cause of 'chaos, and the harm that would befall society were the State not to maintain order' (Charman: 2010, p. 2).

In reality, rigid official control undermines the informal sector. It is doubtful in the present South African economic order if such controls can ever rid the streets of hawkers. Informal economic activity is necessitated by economic marginality. It is a survival strategy. Absent other sources of livelihood, it is highly likely that hawkers will persist trading on the pavements, despite police harassment and fines. They do so out of necessity in order to stay alive. Faced with extortion and other corrupt activities by those in positions of authority, informal traders are forced to oblige the tastes of officialdom rather than lose their sources of livelihood. Corruption thus reproduces and sustains itself as part of the survival strategies of the poor.

Unemployment and lack of skills do enhance reliance on the State. Politicians depend on political office for income, especially when they cannot find employment elsewhere due to a lack of qualifications. The uncertainty of political office encourages corrupt practices to 'build a nest for rainy days'. Poor residents utilise their political support to gain material benefits from the State, in this instance, from councillors. In sum, political support is traded for material benefits.

Patron-client relations have in turn fanned nepotism. It has become accepted as a way of life. This accentuates ethnic identity. One takes care of one's own to ensure that one, too, will be attended to should one fall into hard times. Recruiting one's own is thus a way of providing security to future employment. Meritocracy is eroded.

The qualification is worth repeating, that patron-client relations are not peculiar to the poor and illiterate. Nor should an assumption be made about a causal relationship as such between poverty and patronage. Councillors do prioritise the interests of the wealthy and established business, as well as the 'middle classes'. They discriminate against the poor, whilst promoting established business and wealthy residents. Such policies effectively aid and perpetuate inequality.

For instance, failure to support informal traders not only freezes income-generating possibilities, but also widens inequality. This, in turn, breeds tension. Those who remain poor, while others prosper, are embittered. The bitterness stems from a sense of unfairness. This is especially prevalent where the State is seen to provide preferential access to the rich over the poor to what should be commonly owned natural resources. This is effectively discrimination and, combined with the 'value-chain' of patronage and corruption experienced by the poor, it creates even more bitterness and tension.

Patronage Politics: Impact on Local Politics

Patronage politics must not be understood to be only the domain of the poor. The middle-class and individual business people, through tenders, do partake in patronage politics. The poor use their votes to leverage material benefits from politicians, whilst business people rent out politicians for financial gain. As for politicians, they hand out patronage to win and retain political office, and do also benefit financially.

Albeit an understandable survival strategy, especially on the part of the poor, patronage politics has a corrosive effect on South Africa's body politic. Because it fosters factionalism and social tension, marginalised sections of the community disengage from political institutions and processes. This implies loss of faith in political institutions. Consequently, residents are prone to resort to extra-judicial measures to register concerns and seek remedy. The State is as such, steadily and corrosively, delegitimised, and its authority undermined.

Factionalism also breaks community ties. Residents are divided into winners and losers. Social cohesion suffers. Communities no longer function as a cohesive whole. This presents a challenge for public mobilisation. Societal problems often require collective remedial action, and a community divided presents a challenge to combat societal problems and efforts to build a social compact around a common vision.

Prevalence of patronage politics reduces politics entirely for the fulfilment of instrumental ends. In other words, it downplays the normative values, such as fairness and equality, of the democratic system. This predisposes citizens to tolerate violations of procedures so long as their material needs are met. Democratic culture is thus weakened.

Nepotism, a direct outcome of patronage politics also promotes ethnic identification. This is a particularly dire problem in diverse communities for it fans ethnic tension, which may easily break into full-blown ethnic/racial conflict. Places like Grabouw, for instance, have already experienced full-blown racial conflict amongst Coloureds and Black Africans.

Tension not only results from racial or ethnic tensions, but also from inequality or uneven development. This is because inequality takes a racial form, which suggests a perpetuation of South Africa's past of racial division and its attendant social consequences. Racial hostility has not entirely evaporated. In fact, it is sustained by persistent inequality that is now somewhat aided by patronage politics.

POLICY CONCERNS AND RECOMMENDATIONS

Patronage and other related practices, as discussed above, are a function of history, social institutions and culture: they cannot be easily changed through policy action; that said, there are some social practices that can be influenced through policy actions. And while others are not amenable to policy influence, their impact, nonetheless, on institutions and political behaviour, should thus be highlighted. Based on the foregoing research findings and analysis, the study recommends the following policy actions:

Selection Processes Based on Democracy and Merit

Quite clearly, one of the central interventions required for dealing with the culture and practice of patronage politics pertains to processes that political parties follow to select candidates for local government elections and for management and other positions in this sphere of government. With regard to councillors, all parties represented in these structures (and independent candidates) will argue that their political processes are informed by criteria based on service to the people, including confidence of, and popularity within, the community; capacity to understand policy and how it should be translated into development programmes; some educational qualifications; and so on. Yet, as pointed out in the study, this does not always manifest in actual practice and it raises the question about the rigour and integrity of the selection processes. Further, it is critical to follow both the letter, and the spirit, of statutes that govern recruitment of municipal officials.

Ensuring that Party Members and the Public Generally Know Their Rights

While it is the responsibility of parties to ensure genuine non-partisan service to the public and individual residents, communities at large have an important complementary role to play. When residents and party members know their rights and have the confidence to assert them, it is difficult for crooked leaders and officials to treat them shabbily. There is the need for intensive campaigns to educate party members and the public at large to know, and demand, their rights in internal party processes and services they deserve from municipalities. Related to this are such issues as the effectiveness of ward committees, as well as the integrity of processes to develop integrated development plans. The latter are in most instances developed by consultants, with a modicum of public consultation. Measures such as those proposed some years ago about usage of name tags and posters outlining citizens' rights in front offices – which were hardly implemented – need to be rolled out in earnest.

Eliminate Factionalism Within Parties and Racial/Ethnic Mobilisation in Inter-party Competition

It is in the interest of all genuine political parties that intra- and inter-party contestation is informed by issues of substance. Faction-riven party organisations are unable to debate and resolve issues of policy and coherently articulate these to the public. Critically, if they are elected into office, their ability to meet their mandate is severely circumscribed. While divisions on policy and ideology are the stuff of democratic politics, this is different from groupings coalescing around the dispensing of patronage. Besides the many adverse consequences for the parties and the public outlined in this report, factional patronage politics has the tendency to attract crooks who, by mimicking and exaggerating factional conspiracies, entrench themselves in parties and aggravate poor service delivery. Others divisively seize on identities of race, ethnicity, language, and places of birth as the currency of political mobilisation.

Campaign Against Corruption at All Levels and in All Sectors

It is necessary to ensure the integrity of systems and structures set up to deal with patronage, maladministration and corruption. It should be obvious to the councillors and the officials that there are consequences to a failure to meet the requirements of the country's laws and other requirements of public administration. This should apply equally to the private sector. Provincial and national spheres of government – which are populated by individuals who in terms of party hierarchies are regarded as senior cadres – should act and be seen to act as a force of example. The unedifying accounts of similar or even more serious misdemeanours in the other spheres of government do not inspire confidence among lower structures of parties. Over time, patronage and general misconduct can be internalised as the norm, impoverishing the entire body politic.

Enforcement of Accountability

Tolerance of mediocrity is partly reinforced by a relative lack of consequences for incompetence or poor performance. The Auditor General's latest municipal audit report highlights this as a worrying trend. A similar concern was raised in last year's report: officials are simply not sanctioned for wrongdoing, it is as if malfeasance is condoned, which shows a failure of oversight or unwillingness to hold wrongdoers accountable, and institutional performance consequently suffers; only by exercising accountability and applying sanctions where they are warranted, can this be averted.

Promote Integrity of Public Institutions

Violation of rules undermines the integrity of institutions. This creates space for abuse of power and resources. The consequence is not only the failure of public institutions to live up to their mandate, but also recourse to violence. Where individuals feel failed by rules or are bullied by those in positions of influence, they lose faith in the institution and take matters into their own hands. There have already been instances of municipal council meetings breaking out in violence, even shooting, in Eastern Cape's Lusikisiki, for instance. This is alarming and needs to be curbed. One way is simply to ensure that officials and politicians stick to the rules. Adherence to rules ensures that everyone is treated fairly and institutions are likely to perform as intended. This will reinforce a culture of respect for rules, from which our society can only benefit.

Informal Sector: From Nuisance to an Economic Activity

The informal sector presents an opportunity to the unemployed to make a living and accumulate an income: it not only frees them from state dependency, but has the potential to catapult them into sustainable economic activity. Local government structures must review policies towards informal traders. Rather than placing too high a premium on artificial, aesthetic notions of a town/city, policy makers should prioritise the economic upliftment and self-sufficiency of its citizenry. The country has more to gain from a relatively self-sufficient citizenry than from streets without hawkers.

Small Traders: Organisational Mobilisation

It appears that small and/or informal traders are relatively unorganised. This partly explains why officialdom does not heed their concerns. Sectors and interest groups are more effective as an organised force than as individual voices. Informal traders must be encouraged to mobilise themselves into effective organisations. This will not only give them numerical strength, but will also draw in various forms of expertise and competence they can utilise towards their objectives. The inability of established small traders to compete with immigrant peers, for instance, is reflective of poor organisation, infrastructure, and systems to source merchandise collectively, and thus use economies of scale to negotiate lower wholesale prices.

Proximity of Social Services

Proximity of social services determines access. Oftentimes they are required to use public transportation to reach centres where state services are provided. This demands money they often do not have. For services aimed at the poor, it makes sense that they are located within their place of residence. Some departments, especially SASSA, have received praise for their accessibility, but others remain distant from where people live. If a permanent structure cannot be built, then adequate, more regular and predictable mobile services should be provided.

Official Communication: Public and Community Radio

Poor people rely on radio both for entertainment and as a source of information. Radio is not only cheap, but it is accessible to the overwhelming majority in languages that people understand, including local dialects in the case of community radio. There are parts of the country, however, that do not have access to signals of public service radio channels, and do not have community radio stations. This denies poor people useful public information that may make a difference in their lives. The public broadcaster should ensure that no part of our country suffers from this deficiency. If not all channels, the dominant language in any given community should be accessible on radio. Information can make a huge difference to the lives of citizens. Radio eliminates the problem of distance and time. Messages communicated through radio are received instantly, and thus generate quick, if not immediate, response.

Address the Corrosive Effect of Nepotism on Social Cohesion

Nepotism erodes community ties. It leads to people shunning the different 'other' and associating with their 'own'. This undermines a sense of community built around common residence or even political association. Although it is an understandable consequence of survival, nepotism nonetheless has a dire impact, not only on the health of South Africa's political life, but also on the quality of public institutions.

Nepotism may not easily lend itself to elimination through policy action, but the practice itself can be discouraged through exemplary public behaviour and credible messaging. Public appointments should be made in a way that underscores the importance of merit. This includes removing individuals who lack demonstrable competence for jobs in which they are employed. The Auditor General's municipal reports for the last two years, including this year's report, reveal countless instances of individuals employed in positions for which they have no skills. Nothing has happened to remedy such inappropriate appointments. Instead, consultants have been hired, at huge cost to the fiscus, to perform functions for which individuals have been employed. Tolerance of mediocrity implies that merit does not count, and when this becomes a popular belief in society, the legitimacy of the State and the democratic system suffers. Once this sets in, it will take generations to reverse.

Resolve the Issue of Party Political Funding

Secretive contributions to political party coffers present fertile ground for patronage and deeper manifestations of corruption. Besides the fact that liaisons of this kind lend themselves to all manner of temptations (fund-raisers taking and concealing 'cuts' of the donation, for example), with the organisational principal unsighted, many benefactors do directly or by implication suggest or expect paybacks. The fundraisers themselves do hint at 'prosperity' that would somehow befall the donors for their generosity. As indicated earlier, this descends to a level where business people identify and back specific candidates for senior positions with the expectation that the candidate's success would advantage their enterprise. This has the effect of eroding democratic principles within parties and across society.

It may well be time for South Africa to take the plunge and allocate more public resources to political parties in accordance with existing formulae, which can be 'tweaked' to take into account factors such as parties that are not represented in legislatures. To supplement the public coffers for such allocations, a Fund for the Promotion of Democracy could be established, to which contributions at an agreed threshold can be made.

BIBLIOGRAPHY

African National Congress. (n.d.). 'Leadership Renewal, Discipline and Organisational Culture'. Available at: www.anc.org.za (Accessed: 10 August 2013).

African National Congress. (2010). 'Report of the 3rd National General Council held at the Durban Exhibition Centre Durban/Thekwini'. Available at: www.anc.org.za (Accessed: 07 August 2013).

ANC, (2012). 'Task-Team Report: Investigation into Irregularities and Manipulation of List processes – May 2011 Local Elections', Press Statement.

Auditor General South Africa. (2012). Consolidated General Report on the Local Government Audit Outcomes of 2011–2012. Copyright 2013 by Auditor General of South Africa.

Ake, C. (1993). The Unique Case of African Democracy. *International Affairs*, 69 (2). Pp. 239–244.

Bates, R. H. (1973). Modernisation Ethnic Competition and the Rationality of Politics in Comtemporary Africa. In: Rothschild, D. & Olunsorola (eds) 1982. *State versus Ethnic Claims: African Policy Dilemmas*. Boulder, Colorado: Westview Press.

Blanton, R., Mason, D. & Athow, B. (2001). Colonial Style and Post-Colonial Ethnic Conflict in Africa. *Journal of Peace Research* , Vol 38, pp. 473–491.

Bearfield, D. A. (2009). 'What is Patronage? A Critical Reexamination', in *Public Administration Review*, pp. 64–74.

Besley, T. & Maitreesh, G. (2006). 'Public Goods and Economic Development'. In Abhijit, V., et al., eds. (2006). *Understanding Poverty*, Oxford: Oxford University Press. Pp. 286–301.

Charman, A. (2012). *Is informality being disallowed by government?*. Econ 3 3, 11 November. Available at: http://www.econ3 3.org/article/informality-being-disallowed (Accessed: 04 July 2013).

Chipkin, I. & Meny-Gibert, S. (2012). 'Why the Past Matters: Studying Public Administration in South Africa', *Journal of Public Administration*, 47 (1), pp. 1–12.

Craig, C. (1993). 'Nationalism and Ethnicity', *A Review of Sociology*, Vol.19, pp. 211–239.

David, B. (1991). *Africa in History: Themes and Outlines*. London: Phoenix Press.

Department of Co-Operative Governance and Traditional Affairs (2012). 'Service Delivery Protests: Trends from 2004 to June 2012'. A paper delivered at the ANC's Governance and Legislature Workshop, DBSA, Midrand, 17–18 August 2012.

Fanon, F. (1961). *The Wretched of the Earth*. New York: Grove Press.

Freedman, A. (1988). 'Doing Battle with the Patronage Army: Politics, Courts, and Personnel Administration in Chicago' in *Public Administration Review*, 48 (5) pp. 847–859.

Fukuyama, F. (2011). *The Origins of Political Order: From Prehuman Times to the French Revolution*. London: Profile Books.

Gibbs, T., (2011). 'A Symposium on Comparative Internal Perspectives on Public Sector

Reform'. Paper delivered on Bantustan Legacies: Provincial Government Policies (as seen on the ground) Since 1994', Johannesburg: Public Affairs Research Institute and the Innovations for Successful Societies Programme, January 2011.

Gump, W. R. (2000). 'The Functions of Patronage in American Party System: An Empirical Reappraisal', *Midwest Journal of Political Science*, 15 (1) pp. 87–107.

Hyslop, J. (2005). 'Political corruption before and after apartheid', *Journal of Southern African Studies*, 32 (4).

Hosking, G. (2000). 'Patronage and the Russian State'. *The Slavonic and East European Review*, 78(2), pp. 301–320.

Johnston, M.(1979), 'Patrons and Clients, Jobs and Machines: A Case Study of the Uses of Patronage', *The American Political Science Review*, 73(2).

Kroeger, A. M. (2012). 'Patronage and Public Goods Provision in Africa', Theses, Dissertations and Student Scholarship, paper 16, Lincoln, Nebraska: University of Nebraska.

Kopecky, P. (2011). 'Political Competition and Party Patronage: Public Appointments in Ghana and South Africa'. Political Studies, 59 (39), pp. 713–732.

Leibbrant, M. & Finn, A. (2012). *Inequality in South Africa and Brazil: Can we trust the numbers.* Centre for Development and Enterprise (CDE) Insight, July 2012. Available at: http: www.cde.org.za/publications/india-brazil (Accessed 10 July 2013).

Local Government Sector Education (LGSETA). (2011). LGSETA Councillor Information and Profiles 2011 (pdf). Available at: ww.lgseta.co.za (Accessed: 01 July 2013).

Mamdani, M. (1996). *Citizen and Subject: Contemporary Africa and the Legacy of Late Colonialism.* Princeton, New Jersey: Princeton University Press.

Maxabella Pty Ltd. (n.d.). Maxabella Luxury Homes and Tigme.com. Available at: www.maxabella.co.za (Accessed: 07 October 2013).

Munro, W. (1996). Power, Peasants and Political Development: Reconsidering State Construction in Africa. *Comparative Studies in Society and History*, 38 (1), pp. 112–148.

Mwenda, A. M. & Tangri, R. (2005). 'Patronage Politics, Donor Reforms and Regime Consolidation in Uganda', *African Affairs*, 104(416).

Netshitenzhe, J. (2012). *Competing Identities of a National Liberation Movement versus Electoral Party Politics: Challenges of Incumbency.* www.mistra.org.za, 31 May. Available at: http://www.mistra.org.za/mediadocs/competing%201Identities.pdf (Accessed 12 September 2013).

Neocosmos, M. (2008). *The Politics of Fear and the Fear of Politics.* 05 June. Available at : http://www.abahlali.org/node/3616 (Accessed 10 June 2013).

Neocosmos, M. (2011). 'Transition, Human Rights, Violence: Rethinking a Liberal Political Relationship in the African Neo-Colony', *A Journal for and about Social Movements*, Volume 3 (2): 359–399.

News24. (2009). 'ID Suicide: Joy Over House'. *News24 Online*, 26 November. Available at http://www.news24.com (Accessed 01 September 2013).

Picard, L. (2005). *The State of the State: Institutional Transformation, Capacity and Political Change in South Africa.* Johannesburg: Wits University Press.

Scott, J. C. (1969). 'Corruption, Machine Politics and Political Change', *The American Political Science Review*, 63(4), pp. 1142–1158.

Scott, J. C. (2005). *Patronage Regimes and American Party Developments From the Age of*

Jackson to the Progressive Era. United Kingdom: Cambridge University Press.

Schlesinger, A. M. (1945). *The Age of Jackson*. Boston, Massachusetts: Little, Brown and Company.

Seoposengwe, M. (2012). 'Circumstances at Birth Are Important Drivers of Inequality in South Africa', 24 July. Available at: http://www.worldbank.org/en/news/pressrelease/ 2012/07/24/circumstances-birth-important-drivers-inequality-south-africa (Accessed: 05 July 2013).

Solow, R. (1957). 'Technical Change and the Aggregate Production Function', *The Review of Economics and Statistics*, 39,(3), pp. 312–320.

Sorauf, J. F. (1959). 'Patronage and Party', *Midwest Journal of Political Science*, 3(2), pp. 115–126.

Sorauf, J. F. (1960). 'The Silent Revolution in Patronage', *Public Administration Review*, 20(1), pp. 28–34.

Szeftel, M. (1987). 'The Crisis in the Third World'. In: Bush, R., Johnston, G. & Coates, D. eds. 1987. *The World Order: Socialist Perspectives*. Oxford Polity Press. pp. 87–141.

Szeftel, M. (2000). 'Between Governance and Underdevelopment: Accumulation and Africa's Catastrophe', *Review of African Political Economy*, 27 (85), pp. 427–441.

Van Onselen, C. (1982). *Studies in the Social and Economic History of the Witswatersrand, 1886–1914, Vol 2: New Nineveh*. London: Longman.

Von Holdt, K. (2011). Cosatu members and strike violence: what we learn from quantitative and qualitative data. In: Buhlungu, S. & Tshoaedi, M. ed. 2013. *Analysing the results of COSATU*. Social Sciences Ebooks. Online Collection 2013, pp: 186–211.

Wallerstein, E. (1973). Class and Class-Conflict in Contemporary Africa. *Canadian Journal of African Studies*, 7 (3), pp. 375–380.

Ward, P. M. (1998). 'International Forum on Regularization and Land Markets'. *Land Lines Newsletter of Lincoln Institute of Land Policy*, 10 (4).

Wilson, J. Q. (1961). 'The Economy of Patronage'. *The Journal of Political Economy*, 4(69), pp. 369–380.

Wrong, M. (2001). *It's Our Turn to Eat: The Story of a Kenyan Whistle-Blower*. Harper Collins: Great Britain.

Young, C. (2004). 'The end of post-colonial state in Africa? Reflections on changing African Political Dynamics', *African Affairs*, 103 (410), pp. 23–49.

INDEX

accountability need 131–132

Affordable Land & Housing Data Centre (ALDC) 97

African National Congress (ANC),
cadre deployment 23–24;
election task team 118–119;
Mafikeng Conference (1997) 16;
service delivery protests 16, 101;
Stellenbosch Conference (2002) 16;
weakness 19

Arabella Country Club 81–82

Arap Moi, Daniel 30, 44

Area Study and Discipline: A Useful Controversy? 48

Auditor General's report (2010–2011) 15–16, 122, 131, 134

Bantustan system 36–37

Bates, Robert 48–49

Bearfield, D. A. 25, 29–31, 38

Besley, T. 32

Bongi, *Mme* 118

Calhoun, Craig 42

careerism 19–20

case studies *see* Diepsloot; Hermanus; Kleinmond; Maluti-A-Phofung Mhlontlo Municipality; Nketoana Municipality; Overstrand; Petsana

Chipkin, I. 36–37

Citizen and Subject 35

citizenship meaning 41–42

class issues 57, 124

Community Development Workers (CDW) 67–68

Community Police Forum (CPF) 99–100

competitive politics 43–44, 49

consultant usage 16, 134

co-operatives 95–96, 125–126

corruption, campaign against 131

Dalmar, Mr 88–89

Davidson, Basil 36

'*dedel abanye*' principle 19–20

Diasy, testimony 86

Diepsloot 52;
Community Development Workers 67–68;
Community Police Forum (CPF) 99–100;
cultural issues 89;
description 53;
economic structure 64;
electoral disputes 120;
electricity issues 97;
foreign-born traders 86–88, 92, 124;
gender issues 70;
health care 97;
housing 97;
informal traders 84, 126–127;
institutional framework 56;
job creation 111;
job situation 68–72;
labour recruitment officers 70;
Local Development Forum 70–71, 73;
nepotism 73;
North-West Township (NORWETO) Chamber of Commerce 88, 90;
Operation Hlasela 111;
organisational mobilisation 70;
People's Housing Process (PHP) 97;
policing issues 98–99;
politicians' rivalry 106–107;
Proof of Residence 111, 116;
protest against 70-72, 115;
radio stations 77;
rent-seeking 89–90, 92;
service delivery issues 100–101, 111;
social assistance 67;
social services 97;
state role 63, 96–97;
violence 68

Dlamini-Zuma task team 119, 121

Donald, testimony 87
Dube, Martin 91
Dube, Mervis 91
Eastern Cape selection as case study 50
    see also Mhlontlo Municipality
electoral issues 24, 37–38, 113, 118–120;
    130
ethnicity 37, 117 see also foreign-born;
    xenophobia factionalism 129, 131
Fikile 109
Finn, A. 31
fishing issues 56, 92–95, 126
foreign-born, competition with 68–69,
    133;
    education levels 69;
    labour 69–70, 124;
    movements against 70–71;
    sexism 88
Free State selection as case study 50
    see also Maluti-A-Phofung;
    Nketoana Municipality
Fukuyama, Francis 24, 36
Fund for the Promotion of Democracy
    134
Gauteng selection as case study 50
    see also Diepsloot
Gibbert, S. Meny- see Meny-Gibbert, S.
Giyose, Mandisa 102
Grabouw racial conflict 129
Grail Centre Trust 69
Guqa, Handsome Yongama 68
Hermanus, housing 75–76;
    job competition 72;
    land issues 79–81;
    racism 74–75, 81;
    social assistance 66
housing 76, 78
Hyslop, J. 36
inequality 46–47, 78–79, 129;
    Africa 33–37;
    Brazil 31;
    Hermanus 79;
    SA 32, 36–37
informal traders 84;
    failure to support 127;

municipal interaction 84–85, 125,
    127;
    organisational mobilisation 70,
    132–133
It's Our Turn to Eat: The Story of a Kenyan
    Whistle-Blower 44
Jackson, Andrew 26–27
Jikijela, Mzimkhulu Jeremiah 102–104,
    118–119, 121–122
Johannesburg Development Agency
    (JDA) 72
Johnston, M. 29
Kenya, corruption 44;
    patronage positive aspects 30
Khel, Maghdud 91
Kibaki, Mwai, 30, 44
Kithongo, John 44
Klate, Olivier 69
Kleinmond, foreign-born employment
    69
Kopecky, P. 31
Kroeger, A. M. 33
Kruger, Paul 30–31
legislation 16–17
Leibbrant, M. 31
local government 15–16, 23, 50;
    knowledge of rights 130–131;
    protest 41, 57–58;
    reform 37
Local Government Sector for Education
    and Training (LGSETA) 118
Mahlangu, Madlozi 88
Maile, Isaac 70
Maitreesh, G. 32
Makhubela, Rogers 70, 107, 111
Maluti-A-Phofung, dependence on state
    95;
    description 55;
    economic structure 62;
    institutional framework 55
Mamdani, Mahmood 35–36
Mashonisa 19, 125
Mathebula, Dennis 87–88
Mbikwana, Mzolisi 70
Meny-Gibbert, S. 36–37

Mexico transformation politics 42–44
Mhlobo, Wezile 68
Mhlongo, Skhumbuzo 115
Mhlontlo Municipality,
    community development workers 68;
    dearth of self-employment 92;
    description 54;
    economic structure 62–63;
    electoral disputes 119–120;
    foreign-born traders 83, 90–91;
    natural resources 126;
    non-attendance at public meetings
        120;
    politicians' rivalry 102–106, 118–122;
    social assistance 65;
    social fissures absence 82;
    subsistence 126;
    traditional authority 55, 120–121
Mlamli, Siyakholwa 102
*Modernization, Ethnic Competition, and
    the Rationality of Politics in
    Contemporary Africa* 49
Monyai, Susan 72
Motshwane, Molly 67–68
Municipal Systems Amendment Act
    (2011) 16–17
Munro, W. 56
Mxinwa, Mzikalimela 103–104, 118–119
National General Council (NGC) 16
Nationalism and Ethnicity 42
natural resource access 64, 81–82, 92–93
Ndlabhu, Lulama 68
Neocosmos, M. 34, 42
nepotism 72–74, 83, 116–117, 122–123,
    129, 133–134
Netshitenzhe, Joel 40
New Babylon, New Nineveh 30
New Public Management (NPM) 37
Nkala, Lefa 70
Nketoana, co-operatives 95–96;
    description 55;
    economic structure 62–63;
    institutional framework 55, 56
Nqatha, Xolile 102
Ofentse testimony 77–78

Oletta testimony 93–94
Olivia testimony 93–94
Operation Hlasela 111
Overstrand 54
    attitude to foreign-born 117;
    description 54;
    economic structure 63;
    Fishers Forum 92;
    fishing rights 56, 92–94, 126;
    institutional framework 56–57;
    job situation 69
    municipal attitudes 83;
    natural resources 126;
    racism 94–95, 126;
    sexism 94;
    state role 63
Paballo Co-operatives 95
Paballo, *Mme* testimony 95–96
Palesa, *Mme* testimony 108–109
Partido Accion Nacional (PAN) (Mexico)
    43
Partido del la Revolución Democrática
    (PRD) (Mexico) 43
Partido Revolucionoria Institucional
    (PRI) (Mexico) 43–44
patron-client relationship 18, 23, 101, 116,
    127
patronage politics 114;
    ANC 16;
    causes 48;
    corrosive effect 129;
    definition 15, 20, 23;
    economic status 112;
    educational aspects 39–40;
    electoral recommendations 130;
    electoral support 113;
    ethnographic research methodology
        48;
    feudalism 24–25;
    history 24;
    housing 100;
    inequality perpetuation 30;
    institutional aspects 46, 129;
    job creation 121;
    local government *see* local

government, municipality concerned;
  manifestation 57–58, 61;
  Medieval Europe 24–25;
  middle class participants 129;
  policing 100;
  positive aspects 31;
  strong-man concept 19;
  styles 38–39;
  Transvaal Republic 31;
  USA 24–29
Petsana, budget debacle 107–110;
  co-operatives 125–126;
  dearth of self-employment 92;
  dependence on state 95;
  social fissures absence 82
Picard, L. 36
Plunkitt, George Washington 37
political office as income generation 118,
  127
political parties, competition 111–112;
  donors 15, 30, 134;
  electoral support 24, 37–38, 118-119;
  party system 17–19;
  recruitment issues 27–28;
  reform aspects 20, 38
Pontsho, *Mme* 109
poverty aspects 17, 28–30, 39–40, 45–46,
  49–50, 64
poverty/inequality correlation 47, 61, 113
public institutions,
  integrity promotion 132;
  relationship 18–19, 122
Puleng, *Mme* 110
racism 77–78, 81, 94–95, 126, 129;
  fishing industry 94–95;
  Hermanus 74–75;
  political parties 111–112
radio 77, 116;
  access 133;
  Xhosa 77
rent-seeking 124
Scott, J. C. 26–31
Seale, Samuel 107
Semela, *Councillor* 109, 118
Seoposengwe, Mmenyane 31–32

September, Oliphant 65
service delivery issues 16–17, 23, 40,
  100–101, 111, 123
Seswane, Oscar 69
sexism 88;
  fishing industry 93–94;
  Overstrand 94
Shermarke, Maxamed 90
social grants 96
social mobilisation 56–57
social services 113;
  accessibility 133;
  Hermanus 75–76;
  lack of delivery 121
socio-economic relevance 18
Solow, R. 33
Somali Forum of Traders 88
Sondaba, Monde 103
Sorauf, Frank 25–26, 29, 38
South African National Civic
  Organisation (Sanco) 100–101
South African Social Security Agency
  (SASSA) 66, 133
spaza shops *see* informal traders
state assistance,
  dependence on 83, 115, 127;
  informal traders 85–86
  state assistance *see also* municipality
  concerned
Swanepoel, Susan 92
Szeftel, Morris 29, 33–34, 37
taxi industry 19;
  Zwelihle testimony 76
The Employment Bureau of Africa (Teba)
  62
traditional authorities 55–56
Umhlobo Wenene 77
Van Onselen, Charles 30
Van Wyk, Orbert 93
Venter, Stephanie 110
Vondo, Chris 70
Von Holdt, Karl 40–42
Wallerstein, Emmanuel 57
Ward, P. M. 43-44
welfare state 38

Western Cape selection as case study
  50–52
  see also Overstrand
World Bank 31
Wrong, Michela 44
xenophobia 40–42, 124
Young, Crawford 33
Zwane, Phindi 107–108